The Contemporary
Spanish Novel, 1939–1975

Twayne's World Authors Series

Spanish Literature

Janet Pérez, Editor

Texas Tech University

TWAS 752

The Contemporary Spanish Novel, 1939–1975

By Margaret E. W. Jones

University of Kentucky

Twayne Publishers • Boston

The Contemporary
Spanish Novel, 1939–1975

Margaret E. W. Jones

Copyright © 1985 by G. K. Hall & Company
All Rights Reserved
Published by Twayne Publishers
A Division of G. K. Hall & Company
70 Lincoln Street
Boston, Massachusetts 02111

Book Production by Elizabeth Todesco

Book Design by Barbara Anderson

Printed on permanent/durable acid-free
paper and bound in the United States of
America.

Library of Congress Cataloging in Publication Data.

Jones, Margaret E. W., 1938–
   The contemporary Spanish novel, 1939–1975.

   (Twayne's world authors series; TWAS 752. Spanish
literature)
   Bibliography: p. 148
   Includes index.
   1. Spanish fiction—20th century—History and criticism.
I. Title.   II. Series: Twayne's world authors series; TWAS 752.
III. Series: Twayne's world authors series. Spanish literature.
PQ6144.J64   1985   863'.6'09   84–13577
ISBN 0–8057–6601–4

Contents

About the Author

Margaret E. W. Jones received the B.A. from New York State College for Teachers at Albany (now SUNY) in 1959 and the M.A. and Ph.D. from the University of Wisconsin (1961 and 1963). She is presently a professor at the University of Kentucky, where she teaches Spanish and has served in various administrative positions (among them, Associate Dean of the Graduate School, 1977–79). She is presently Director of Graduate Studies for the Spanish Graduate Program. Her field of specialization is modern Spanish literature, with emphasis on the contemporary novel and theater. Professor Jones gives undergraduate and graduate courses in this area and has presented papers and written articles and books in the field (among which are *The Literary World of Ana María Matute,* 1970, and the Twayne volume *Dolores Medio,* 1974).

Professor Jones has served on the editorial boards of several professional journals and is active in regional and national professional organizations.

Preface

The post–Civil War Spanish novel is relatively unknown to the international reading public. Few general critical studies are available to the English speaker; most information is either in Spanish or contained in professional journals not as easily accessible to the general reader. Particularly after the emergence of the Spanish American New Novel, with such stellar writers as Gabriel García Márquez, Julio Cortázar, and Carlos Fuentes attracting worldwide attention, American and European critics have shown more curiosity about peninsular Spanish literature of the recent past. This book will attempt to provide an overview for students of Spanish literature and for nonspecialists interested in Spain under Franco.

It is possible to trace a general course of development for the contemporary Spanish novel through an evolution marked by external as well as aesthetic pressures. The political situation has determined to a great extent the choice (or limitations) of subject matter; to a lesser degree it has even been a factor in shaping stylistic trends. For this reason, an introductory chapter will briefly describe major historical and cultural factors of the period so that the reader can understand the framework in which the Spanish novel from 1939 to 1975 appears.

A limited number of themes occur in the novel of this period (among others, the Civil War, childhood and adolescence, criticism on a social or national level, introspection) but the content is infinitely varied through the mode of expression. Perhaps the most efficient way to follow the trajectory of this genre is to study its formal changes. Structure and style have evolved to modify the relationship between reader and text, and to create an affective level that transmits the author's view without necessity of direct intervention. Chapters 2 through 9 will trace this evolution. Each section contains a survey of the literary situation into which the style fits, its possible antecedents, its distinctive characteristics, and the writers associated with it. Titles and material from the works illustrate the theoretical introduction. Finally, a close look at illustrative novels will follow the general remarks. The works chosen are important historically and, in most cases, have the added attraction of being examples of some of the most interesting literature of the period. The analysis will attempt to point out the convergence of the work with the characteristics of the movement, as well as those factors that make it unique.

A final chapter will briefly mention the major exiled writers and the factors that distinguish their literature. To develop this section to any further degree is a task that would require a separate book. Furthermore, although the exiles have in some cases indirectly affected peninsular literature, direct influence on specific literary movements is not easy to document.

I have consciously avoided using only one writer to exemplify trends (with the obvious exception of Martín-Santos). Many of the best-known novelists have changed and developed their style gradually in a series of works, so to say that an author—rather than the work itself—is typical of a movement would be misleading. Cela, Delibes, Matute, and Juan Goytisolo are all examples of writers who have modified their approach to literature: to associate one with a single movement would be inaccurate.

By the same token the demands of space have necessitated a great selectivity in both primary and secondary references. It is hoped that this study will be a preliminary step to more detailed investigations, as well as to enjoyable reading.

Although the quotations in the text are my translations from the Spanish work, titles of English translations of some of the novels are provided for the reader's information. If the English title deviates substantially from the meaning of the original Spanish, I have also added the literal translation.

Primary works in the Selected Bibliography include only those novels analyzed in the text. Since the notes deal with more specific references, the secondary sources in the bibliography mention major or lengthy overviews of the Spanish novel. From these general sources, many of which contain bibliographies, the interested reader can map out a more specific direction to follow.

Finally, this work could never have been written without the help of three nonliterary "sources": the Interlibrary Loan Service at the Margaret I. King Library of the University of Kentucky; a grant from the University of Kentucky Research Foundation for the preparation of this manuscript, and finally, the patience and advice of my husband, Joseph R. Jones, to whom this book is dedicated.

Chronology

1939   End of Spanish Civil War. Military dictatorship established under Francisco Franco.

1942   *La familia de Pascual Duarte* by Camilo José Cela.

1944   *Nada,* by Carmen Laforet, receives the first Nadal Prize. *Mariona Rebull* by Ignacio Agustí. *Nuevas andanzas y desventuras de Lazarillo de Tormes* by Camilo José Cela.

1946   United Nations breaks relations with Spain.

1948   *Viaje a la Alcarria* by Camilo José Cela.

1950   United Nations approves reestablishment of relations with Spain.

1951   Spain enters UNESCO. *La colmena* by Camilo José Cela.

1953   Economic and military agreement with the United States; United States to establish air and naval military bases in Spain; concordat with the Vatican, proclaiming Catholicism as the national religion and giving special privileges to the Church.

1954   *La vida como es* by Antonio Zunzunegui. *Los bravos* by Jesús Fernández Santos.

1955   United Nations votes to admit Spain. *El Jarama* by Rafael Sánchez Ferlosio wins the 1955 Nadal Prize.

1959   Stabilization plan encouraging foreign economic exchange. Formentor Colloquium takes place on Mallorca. *Primera memoria* by Ana María Matute wins the 1959 Nadal Prize.

1960   *La mina* by Armando López Salinas.

1962   *Dos días de setiembre* by José Manuel Caballero Bonald. *Tiempo de silencio* by Luis Martín-Santos.

1966   Press and Printing Law.

1967   *Volverás a Región* by Juan Benet.

1969   Franco designates Juan Carlos as his successor.

1970   *Reivindicación del conde don Julián* by Juan Goytisolo.

1973 Assassination of Luis Carrero Blanco, recently named president and head of government.

1974 Carlos Arias Navarro named premier; announcement of programs of *apertura* ("opening") allowing more freedom in political and other realms.

1975 Francisco Franco dies; Juan Carlos crowned King of Spain.

Chapter One
Setting the Stage: Extraliterary Factors

The decade immediately preceding the Civil War was a time of cultural and political controversy. While various Spanish parties were battling for control of the newly formed Second Republic (inaugurated in 1931) and rapid social transformation was scandalizing the traditional sectors, the cultural picture also kept pace with many changes. The ever-popular mode of realism was applied to current social issues, reflecting the liberal concerns of the intellectuals of the Second Republic. The most famous of the prewar realists is Ramón J. Sender (b. 1902); others worthy of mention are César Arconada, Joaquín Arderíus, and Manuel Domínguez Benavides. Their committed approach to literature offers a marked contrast with the stance of intellectuals of the preceding generation, accused of being escapist because they preferred aesthetic matters and reflective themes.

The Civil War (1936–1939) paralyzed any serious literary activity. The effects of the holocaust were devastating both to winners and to losers; postwar conditions demanded efforts directed toward survival rather than aesthetics. Descriptions of life during this period document hunger, unemployment, lack of housing, reprisals, a general atmosphere of fear, severe economic problems, and isolation from international political and cultural influences. A paper shortage exacerbated the publishing problems. A reversal of the innovative currents that accelerated during the Second Republic now took place.

Leading figures had disappeared from Spain by the end of the war. Among the dead were Miguel de Unamuno, Ramón del Valle-Inclán, Antonio Machado, and Federico García Lorca. Those in exile included Ramón Sender, Max Aub, Francisco Ayala, and many more. The remaining literary personalities were unable to exert the necessary strength to form or inspire the next generation, and survivors of the Generation of 1898, whose prestige might have influenced the younger writers, were in official disfavor.[1]

1

In the years following the war, the Falangist party had control not only of politics, but of culture as well. Censorship policies (see below, pp. 2–4) allowed the suppression of undesirable material—or authors; conversely, the tenets of the current political position were upheld through approved literary channels.[2] Francoist aesthetics are closely allied to other Fascist models: the exaltation of totalitarian principles and the use of propaganda were part of this literature, with the resultant polarization of villains/heroes. A series of novels—often called the "literature of the winners"—extolling the principles of the regime and depicting the losers in the worst possible light appeared at this time. Among these was a novel by Franco himself, published under the pseudonym of Jaime de Andrade (*Raza* [Race], 1940). The literary quality of most of these works was quite poor; in analyzing a typical example (Rafael García Serrano's *La fiel infantería* [The faithful infantry, 1943]) one critic noted its marginal novelistic connection because of the emphasis on documentary evidence.[3]

Within five years a more open-minded attitude began to surface among the Falangist writers associated with the Generation of 1936. These intellectuals published the journal *El Escorial* (1940–1950); the editors were the essayist Pedro Laín Entralgo and the poet Dionisio Ridruejo. Although the rhetoric of Falangism is still present, the editorial policy reveals a serious effort to raise cultural standards: there is a decreased militancy, a greater intellectual orientation, and the relatively impartial criticism of even those who, as political undesirables, had previously been subjects of scathing reviews.

No accurate portrayal of the postwar Spanish cultural scene would be complete without mention of the type of censorship exercised during this period. Information concerning the unusually restrictive policy is still not complete and perhaps never will be,[4] but censorship affected all modes of public communication: theater, movies, public meetings, the press, and any published works, a category that included imported books as well as those published in Spain for export.

The interpretation of censorship regulations shifted depending on the minister in charge. According to Abellán, the government prohibited material on the Roman Catholic Index, and any criticism of the ideology or practices of the regime, including its views on public morality, historiography, or civil order. It did not permit apology for ideologies that were either nonauthoritarian or Marxist and, at first, it suppressed any work or author who was hostile to the regime. Censorship of a novel did not mean that a work would be totally banned; there were many variations on the final verdict, which ran from total suppression to a request for changes or deletions; the censor might ban the book within Spain but allow it for export, authorize only a limited edition of the work, or even confiscate the book after publication. Evidence suggests that the most prevalent form of censorship was not the complete prohibition of a novel; most authors preferred to revise or cut the offending passage rather than not publish the work at all. Finally Abellán notes still another, undocumented result of the censorship mentality: a type of self-regulation on the part of the author himself. This *"autocensura"* was actually a state of mind that was subconsciously responsible for determining the entire composition of the work, thus automatically passing over potentially offensive material.

Among the many changes the censorship laws underwent during the Franco period, the most drastic was the 1966 Press and Printing Law, under Manuel Fraga Iribarne. In effect, it removed the necessity for prior consultation, making this condition optional. The bitter comments of one writer throw some personal light on the policy:

Until very recently, at times of greater and at times of lesser severity, Spanish writers suffered a tasteless, anonymous, frivolous and contradictory antecedent censorship capable of condemning to ostracism without appeal a book that, three months later, might be mysteriously authorized in its entirety. At present, we profit from a new modality, much more tortuous. In key with the new, peculiar and unexpected democratic sentiment, we may publish anything—very well, almost anything—without the necessity of consulting an antecedent censorship. Censorship may come later, as narrow, arbitrary and inconsistent as circumstances then warrant. *After* publication may come the confiscation of a book by the police, suppression of a magazine, the exorbitant fine, perhaps trial and prison. So astutely devised, so flexible are the concepts of the new censorship, that anyone, worthy or not, may fall foul. All may be crime. Anyone guilty. It depends upon who, when and whyfor.

Thus we have passed from the anonymous criteria of unknown censors who would not tolerate the insertion of passages in which, for example, a woman takes a shower or St. Roque is called ugly, to the persecution of publishers.[5]

One of the most pernicious effects of the isolationist policies of the government was to make writers out of favor inaccessible. This affected both foreign and prohibited Spanish authors, including, among others, Joyce, Faulkner, Kafka, and the Spanish exiles. Time and again, writers and critics emphasize the cultural vacuum that characterized the early postwar years, forcing the younger writers to remain outside the mainstream of contemporary intellectual currents.[6] One member of this group of writers summarizes the situation when she says that "[my group] groped around, starting from zero . . . discovering independently, each in his separate way, and mostly by accident, writers who were known in other countries."[7] Even older, more established novelists found inspiration only outside their country: Torrente Ballester stated that he owed the modern orientation of one of his novels, published in 1972, to "having expatriated myself for a number of years and having found, outside Spain, the intellectual stimulation that I did not receive here."[8]

These discouraging conditions were offset in some measure by the institution of various literary prizes, some in generous amounts. Of these, the most prestigious and first chronologically was the Nadal prize (1944), backed by the Destino Publishing Company. Among the better-known prizes are the Premio Planeta (of the Planeta Company) and the Biblioteca Breve award (Seix Barral). Other prizes for the novel not sponsored by publishers are the National Prize for Literature, the Fastenrath award, the Critic's Prize (Premio de la Crítica), and the Miguel de Cervantes award. This does not exhaust the list.[9]

During the last decade of Franco's reign, signs of unrest had become manifest: student demonstrations, the appearance of clergy who allied themselves with the people, dissatisfaction of workers with the government-run unions, and the constant pressure of Basque extremists who sought independence, a pressure that crystallized in terrorist attacks and assassinations. One of the most publicized was the murder of Franco's chosen successor, Luis Carrero Blanco.

Since the 1960s, the growing importance of Spain on the international political scene, the great influx of tourists, and the jobs provided by foreign industry have contributed to a steady rise in the quality of life: housing, per capita income, educational standards—all improved during this period. The supposed moderation of strict censorship in the 1966 Press and Printing Law is one indication of an effort on the part of the government to present a more open and liberal philosophy. Along with this change, a new permission of importation has allowed works by contemporary Italian, French, English, and American novelists to be more readily available, and extra-Spanish literary influences have played a greater part in the literary formation of the youngest writers.

Chapter Two
Continuing Traditions

The dominant novelistic mode following the Civil War was a continuation of traditional realism. For artistic as well as extraliterary reasons, traditional realism was accepted as a serious aesthetic concern through the 1950s: it was always popular with the reading public, and its resultant economic success assured steady publication. The relatively innocuous content was not controversial, an important issue because of the increasing intervention of censorship. In traditional realism, the novelist stands in omniscient relationship to his work, permitting commentaries, digressions, freedom of spatial and temporal movement, selection and scenification without necessity of hiding his presence from the reader. Typically, traditional realism grounds the protagonist solidly within the times in which he lives, considering him both as an individual with unique concerns and as a representative of the group to which he belongs. The novelists did not neglect inner thoughts and emotions, but the exclusive concentration on the psychological development of a single character is displaced because of the wealth of other information in which his formation is embedded. The less stellar position of the main character and the addition of a richly varied cast of minor characters allow for a more panoramic spatial or temporal view.

This increased emphasis on the milieu and its effects on the individual gives rise to a biographical, family-chronicle novel with definite characteristics. Several authors adopt the *roman fleuve* concept of a single long work or a series of novels that, considered as a whole, present an extensive chronological commentary on the life and times of a family. Ignacio Agustí's series collectively entitled *La ceniza fue árbol* (The ashes were once a tree) is one such example. Against the historical and social background, writers present a faithful and exact account of daily activities at home or work. The dialogue reflects local dialect or speech patterns.

Traditional realism is generally associated with the middle class, whose life and manners it portrays and to whom it was directed. Bourgeois orientation affects the choice of character as well. Whether

6

as a more faithful representative of the values involved or because of the obviously greater possibility of reader identification, the main characters in traditional realism are generally drawn from the middle class. The lower classes are often foils for the main characters. They form part of the background material in a historical sense (e.g., labor problems) or a personal sense (the humble origins of the character) or they undergo a parallel experience for reinforcement. The lower class often reflects middle-class mentality lowered a social rung or two. Only later, in the social novel of the 1950s, will the classes meet in an adversarial position as symbols not of a dialectical movement toward a better life but of the breakdown of an entire socioeconomic system.

These novels share themes of common interest that appear frequently: the ambitions of the middle-class citizen for social or economic status, the nouveau riche and his place in the class structure, the condemnation of the materialism that accompanies the acquisition of wealth, the decline of family fortunes through several generations, the directionless life of the *señorito* (son of the rich father). Although these themes could raise serious doubts about Spain's postwar development, authors generally skirt direct criticism to deal with a moral or ethical issue, thus raising the subject to a more abstract level. However, it is not difficult to read disapproval into those novels that deal with contemporary times, although blame is placed on no specific institution or class.

History and the Novel

The reasons for the selection of historical subjects are varied in traditional realism: history may provide a commentary on the present (either as veiled criticism or as revelation of parallels or cyclical implications); it may portray major or minor figures of earlier periods, allowing "intrahistory" to reveal human constants; or it may simply offer an escape from contemporary life, a "period piece," quaint in conception and charmingly and often authentically detailed. This third type was most prevalent following the Civil War: the temporally exotic settings allowed evasion from harsh reality, provided a comforting reaffirmation of traditional social values, and explored topics that were not politically dangerous. In many of these novels, real events may determine, modify, or affect the lives of the fictional protagonists in a way that imbues them with tragic dimensions, particularly from the temporal vantage point of the reader. Galdós's *Episodios nacionales,* five series of novels spanning a seventy-year period, are masterful examples of fictionalized history.[1] The best-known of the postwar historical novels, Agustí's *Mariona Rebull,* offers an excellent example of the techniques of traditional realism.

Mariona Rebull.   Published in 1944, *Mariona Rebull,* by Ignacio Agustí (b. 1913), became one of the successes of the decade;[2] the large number of editions attests to the persistent interest in this type of writing. The book is the first in a series of novels collectively entitled *La ceniza fue árbol* (The ashes were once a tree), which traces the fortunes of the Rius family through several generations, a procedure recalling the *roman fleuve* technique of nineteenth-century authors. The plot centers around the ambitions of Joaquín Rius, owner of a cloth factory in nineteenth-century Barcelona. He represents the rising middle class and aspires to a place in society, which he hopes to attain by marriage to Mariona Rebull, who personifies all of his social designs. When Mariona eventually learns that Joaquín has married her without love, she has an affair with a former suitor. At a gala opening of the Liceo Theater, a terrorist throws a bomb into the crowd; Joaquín desperately searches for Mariona, and finds the bodies of his wife and her lover together in the lover's box.

Beginning with the words "I speak of many years before," Agustí sets the documentary tone in the first pages of *Mariona Rebull,*[3] describing "my city" in historical and industrial terms, furnishing information on church attendance, the factories (where "man was still not considered at the service of the machine" [10]), the new industrial aristocracy, the mode of daily existence, and so on. While providing the necessary background to the subject of the work (the Rius family, their history, habits, and fortune), Agustí simultaneously creates a nostalgic vision of old Barcelona, emphasizing with his insistence on the past tense the fact that these times have now slipped away. His description gives the impression of comfortable stability, solid values, and noble workers, and he continually uses the epoch as his yardstick, returning to it again and again to measure and reaffirm those values he reveres.

The personal drama of the main characters is inextricably woven into the fabric of the times and is determined by the epoch in which they live. The ill-fated marriage of Joaquín and Mariona is possibly the result of circumstances that relaxed social restrictions and provided an opportunity for an ambitious person to marry above his class. Agustí offers a psychological study of motivation. Joaquín, far from being a "villain," is a man caught in a set of circumstances beyond his control. His ambitions and success symbolize the rise of the moneyed bourgeoisie and its search for a place in the upper-class society of Barcelona. His hopes (objectified in his relationship with Mariona), personal problems, and insecurity make him a sympathetic human being. It is the amalgam of human, social, and historical concerns that makes *Mariona Rebull* the outstanding example of the novel of traditional realism in the postwar period. In effect, the greatest merit of the work lies in the dual role the characters play (in a historical documentary and in a fictional drama) as well as in the apt selection of facts or events that add documentary background for the novel (the Exposition of 1888, labor problems, terrorist bombings). Agustí even allows historical fact to supply the ending for *Mariona Rebull:* the famous bombing of the Liceo took place on 7 November 1893.

The other novels of the series (*El Viudo Rius* [Widower Rius, 1945], *Desiderio* [1957], and *19 de julio* [19 July 1965]) continue with the chronicle of Joaquín and Mariona's son, the slow decadence of his class, and the inevitable rise of the militant working class, finally polarized in anarchism versus capitalism. None, however, manages to capture the human interest with the skill and depth of Agustí's first novel.

If one wishes to consider within the definition of "historical" those works that place the emphasis on historical change or period (omitting works dealing strictly with problems contemporary with the writer's), one can see a continuous interest in the historical subject and in the traditional manner of presentation. Miguel Delibes's *Mi idolatrado hijo Sisí* (My beloved son Sisi, 1951) deals with the bourgeoisie of prewar Valladolid; Dolores Medio's Nadal prize-winner *Nosotros los Rivero* (We Riveros, 1953) follows a female protagonist back to the place of her childhood, where she relives the past in prewar Oviedo; José María Gironella's *Los cipreses creen en Dios* (*The Cypresses Believe in God*, 1953) is the moving chronicle of a Gerona family (1933–36); subsequent works in the trilogy, *Un millón de muertos* (*One Million Dead*, 1961) and *Ha estallado la paz* (Peace Has Burst Forth, published in English as *Peace After War*, 1966) follow this family through the early postwar years. All of these writers show the influence of Galdós and his *Episodios nacionales* in some way. Perhaps the most obvious tribute is the ongoing project of Ricardo Fernández de la Reguera and his wife, Susana March, who at present are composing a series entitled *Episodios nacionales contemporáneos*, among them *Héroes de Cuba* (1962), *La semana trágica* (Tragic week, 1966), *El desastre de Anual* (The disaster of Anual, 1968), which continue tracing Spain's history into the twentieth century.

Contemporary Times

Traditional realism did not limit itself exclusively to subjects drawn from the past. A second rough grouping of novels is also apparent within a decade after the Civil War, its time frame contemporary with the lifetime of the author. Analogies point to another Galdosian series: the *Novelas contemporáneas,* which set the protagonist within the social panorama of his times, and deal—as did the historical novels—with the interaction between recent historical events and their effect on the fictional (but representative) protagonists. There is obvious reluctance on the part of the novelists to comment on socially or politically controversial issues, since the wisdom of the "perspective from the future" is not available. Instead, moral judgments or theses take their place, the criticism dealing with broad human values rather than institutions or the politics responsible for creating them. An excellent example of this is Juan Antonio Zunzunegui's *Esta oscura desbandada* (This dark disbandment, 1952), a bleak picture of postwar Madrid, whose poverty and terrible conditions are translated moralistically into materialism and loss of human values.

La vida como es (Life as it is).   The dean of the modern contemporary novel is Juan Antonio Zunzunegui, whose contributions to Spanish fiction began well before the Civil War. One of the most typical examples of traditional realism is his *La vida como es* (1954). A panorama of life in Madrid in the years immediately preceding the proclamation of the Second Republic, it chronicles events in the Lavapiés district through a cross-section of various social levels. Longer, denser, and more complex than *Mariona Rebull, La vida como es* leaves the impression that the main character is really the city rather than any single person, with macrocosmic implications for the national scene.

There is no main plot line in the novel. Zunzunegui interweaves the stories of representative characters, the alternation of the various segments providing opportunity for contrast and, at times, minimal interaction. Benito the tavernkeeper and his wife, Encarna, represent the middle class; Encarna is ambitious and has several love affairs and business ventures before settling down to being a dutiful wife. Enriqueta, a shopgirl, is the eternal victim, whose moral principles contrast sharply with the materialistic interests and selfish behavior of most of the characters. Cotufas and his family represent the criminal world, which the novelist chronicles in great detail. Myriad thumbnail sketches of other secondary characters afford structural parallels and latitude for indirect commentary on the situations of the more prominent figures.

The sheer number of vignettes indicates the vastness of Zunzunegui's social panorama. His very obvious participation holds the pieces together: asides, direct comments, and especially the addition of good-natured irony, which pervades much of the novel, keeps his presence alive in the reader's mind. However, a more serious note is present in all levels of narration: the emphasis on money and lack of charity gives the impression of a social system whose values have become bankrupt, where vice rather than virtue is rewarded, and where a kind of natural selection provides the direction for society. For example, Enriqueta's decency is contrasted with the cynicism of a coworker whose loveless affair with their employer is directly related to her job security. She succeeds in marrying the man, thus assuring herself a comfortable life. Another girl whose family ties parallel those of Enriqueta escapes from her miserable life by running off with a rich man. Enriqueta, however, refuses to follow either option, and as a result loses her job and at the end of the novel is slowly dying of tuberculosis, existing only on charity. Such obvious contrast serves a clear moral purpose, providing a picture of a society essentially devoid of values. The "message" of the work resides on this level, and the national implications are clear in the offhand remarks of the characters themselves: "This place is full of rogues and beggars . . . Madrid's history is that of Spain. . . ."[4]

Although *La vida como es* fits within the mode of the Galdosian realistic tradition, another Spanish source adds an interesting dimension. The most unusual aspect of the novel is its graphic presentation of the criminal element in Madrid. The details, anecdotes, and ironic humor with which Zunzunegui exposes this stratum recall Cervantes's techniques, especially in the novella *Rinconete y Corta-*

dillo—an influence the author himself acknowledges. Critics have commented on the darker side of life as represented by these people, apparent not so much in the actual robberies as in individual behavior, such as the cruelty with which Cotufas treats his wife. However sinister these characters may appear at the outset, the more Zunzunegui delves into their life and customs, the clearer it becomes that this seemingly classless group is a tightly structured social system. In fact, it is the structural parallel of the bourgeoisie and its value system: pride in work well done, admiration for the "Master," the thieves' school, the importance of maintaining one's honor, a peculiarly consistent code of right and wrong, a "work ethic," and so on. The final impression is of an orderly group with contemporary values (albeit lowered to an amoral level). There is minimal emphasis on poverty, misery, and ruthlessness generally associated with the underworld.

Materialism is a constant theme in Zunzunegui's novels, and *La vida como es* is no exception: money is a prime factor of motivation (either for survival or as an acquisitive urge). Money is equivalent to power, and characters often resort to unethical means to obtain it. Yet Zunzunegui's most serious indictment is evident in the behavior of two minor characters: Cotufas's wife commits suicide rather than be coerced into a life of crime; Enriqueta, the victim shopgirl, is obviously doomed. Their untimely deaths suggest that good people cannot survive in a materialistic society with selfish values.

The Neopicaresque Mode

The revival of the picaresque tradition in the postwar novel is further indication of the literary tendency of turning to the past for inspiration. Since its introduction in the sixteenth century, the picaresque novel has been periodically revived and reinterpreted in such works as the eighteenth-century *Vida* of Torres Villarroel and some of Pío Baroja's works.[5] Assiduously cultivated in the postwar era, the archly naive commentaries of the modern *pícaro* offered a refreshing perspective from which to view modern reality. Contemporary writers adhere to enough of the superficial trappings of the mode to make it easily recognizable: the episodic structure held together by the wanderings of the antihero whose humble origins begin an odyssey of poverty and hunger, the memoir format, the critical, satirical tone, and the questioning attitude of the outsider who must live by his wits are characteristic of old and new versions, but the contemporary adaptations include decidedly modern touches, producing a sort of hybrid, experimental variation of the prototype.

The first obvious contribution to the modern picaresque was written by Camilo José Cela (b. 1916). His *Nuevas andanzas y desventuras de Lazarillo de Tormes* (New sallies and misadventures of Lazarillo de Tormes, 1944) uses the same episodic structure, first-person narrator, and general characterisics as cited above. However, the focus shifts from trickster to victim, for Lazarillo is constantly taken advantage of, and, unlike the prototype, he does not retaliate. He is often duped, and the few positive relationships he has are soon truncated.

While Cela deserves credit for the postwar revival of the picaresque, there are many others who have continued the tradition. Doubtless the most famous of the group is Darío Fernández Flórez's *Lola, espejo oscuro* (*Lola, A Dark Mirror*, 1950). Lola is a beautiful prostitute whose memoirs reveal an ambivalence toward men and a naive approach to life; she describes experiences of the most varied kinds. The titillating nature of the novel made it one of the hits of 1950, although it is not an erotic novel in any sense of the word. More traditional approaches to the genre are Zunzunegui's *El Chiplechandle* (The ship's chandler, 1940), a chronicle of the rise of a poor Spaniard set against the background of a society in moral decay, and Juan Sebastián Arbó's *Martín de Caretas* (1955), which follows the experiences of a boy through life in a rural town to his adventures in the city. Finally, a boldly experimental version of the genre appears in Rafael Sánchez Ferlosio's *Industrias y andanzas de Alfanhuí* (Labors and wanderings of Alfanhuí, published as *Alfanhuí*, 1951), a strange and beautiful combination of minute description with fantastic episodes, whose universal significance removes it from the grim contemporary perspective of the other narrations.

Although these are the most illustrative because they adhere most closely to the original mode, any number of other novels use picaresque elements to their advantage, continuing the national tradition through single episodes, atmosphere, intertextuality, or narrative point of view. Novelists even call attention to their affiliations with the genre: Zunzunegui's own subtitle to *La vida como es* reads "Picaresque Novel in Very Clear Spanish" and critics have naturally associated the work with the genre, even describing it as a novel of "collective roguery."[6] Zunzunegui calls *El chiplechandle* "picaresque action." Cela's prototype even borrows the name of the original *pícaro*, and the other authors mentioned above also spell out parallels or influences. Whether the underlying spirit of the picaresque was retained or whether the modern novelist used only the most obvious formal elements of the genre, it is an interesting fact that the picaresque mode has survived with modifications as one of the constants of Spanish literature.

Chapter Three
Tremendismo

The 1940s saw a change of direction for the Spanish novel with the publication of two key works that inaugurated a deviation from the still popular traditional realism: Camilo José Cela's *La familia de Pascual Duarte* (*The Family of Pascual Duarte*, 1942), a novel so controversial that it was said to have had a thousand critics and only three hundred purchasers,[1] and Carmen Laforet's (b. 1921) *Nada* (Nothing, published as *Andrea*, 1944). Both novels were best-sellers, a sign that the public was culturally and intellectually ready for a fresh interpretation of realism in Spanish letters. The name of this new movement is *tremendismo*.

In *tremendismo*, stylistic and structural devices transmit the author's view to the reader, in contrast with the direct presence of the novelist in traditional realism. Characteristic of these novels is the accumulation of episodes or descriptions that range from unpleasant to disgusting, literary procedures that cause the "tremendous" effect on the reader that gave the movement its name. An emphasis on violence, death, misery, poverty, illness, pain, unhappiness, and anguish fosters an atmosphere of tension and anxiety throughout the works.

The contrast with the more moderate tone of the traditional novel could not have been more marked. Cela, who vigorously denied his role as initiator of *tremendismo,* correctly points out that the seamier side of life has long been present in Spanish literary tradition—in fact, he stated that it is as old as Spanish literature itself, mentioning the picaresque novel and Quevedo as proof.[2] He could have added later naturalism and authors like Valle-Inclán. However, each period, movement, or individual writer directs these elements to specific, often different ends, and *tremendismo* is no exception.

Like traditional realism, *tremendismo* draws on everyday reality as a basis for the work, but where the conventional novel explores the social milieu through detailed, enumerative descriptions of exterior reality, a panoramic scene, and representative characters, *tremendismo* chooses an individual protagonist with a unique, atypical point of view to reveal patterns of universal behavior rather than (or as well as) social modes. The shift of focus from the traditional novel to *tremendismo* becomes apparent in the preeminence of the individual viewpoint. The new manner of presentation displaces the analysis of social, exterior factors in favor of a study of the character's psychological state in reaction to external stimuli. This inner dimension often runs separately but parallel to the course of outer events (the "story"[3]). The movement of the plot derives from inner developments, often a coming-to-terms, a search for authenticity or for a meaning in one's life, and may consequently invert, fragment, or disregard chronological sequence. Feeling of unease, resentment, unhappiness, fear, even anguish—the negative side of the emotional scale—plague the character, who in turn colors the tone of the work and interprets most situations in a pessimistic way. This attitude has led many critics to interpret *tremendismo* in its socially critical function, as a reflection of the grim conditions of postwar Spain and of the misery of those subjected to them.[4]

The main character is likely to be an antihero in several aspects: he offers no outstanding or exemplary traits—in fact, he may be a failure. Because of his own attitude and the impressions he gleans from his surroundings, the world seems menacing, hostile, and even absurd to the *tremendista* character. Estrangement and alienation from life are the natural consequence, and the resultant isolation allows neither respite for unburdening himself nor hope for communication with others. Thus all decisions and actions are effected in complete solitude, and the responsibility for these acts rests squarely on the protagonist.

The secondary characters who populate these novels exhibit such negative or antisocial traits that the reader must conclude that this behavior is a natural part of the fabric of everyday life. Prostitutes, mental cases, criminals, hypocrites, and failures are the contacts from whom the main character justifiably draws his black outlook on the world. Rejection and deliberate mental and physical cruelty mark even family relationships. Rebellion against accepted social behavior is evident not only in acts of overt defiance but on a lexical plane, where elegant, neutral language is discarded in favor of a more popular, earthy speech peppered with slang, blasphemy, strong interjections, references to sex, bodily functions, and so forth. While the introduction of this characteristic (particularly in Cela) is a major technical innovation that supports the anguish of the character, less talented imitators have exaggerated these traits to the point of sensationalism.[5]

These novels are set in the contemporary period and contain allusions to specific places or events, but the movement inward endows them with a mythic, atemporal quality that makes constructs of behavior more significant than social criticism. For that reason a case can be made for a connection between *tremendismo* and existentialism. Chronologically, *tremendismo* roughly parallels French existentialism: Sartre's works date from the 1930s on, and the fictional interpretations by Sartre himself and by Camus were published in this period. Existentialism rejects philosophical abstractions, preferring instead to consider man within a concrete situation. The existential hero (or antihero) feels out of step with contemporary reality, where both objects and people confirm his idea of the absurdity of existence. His lack of communication particularly and the threat of the "other" cause loneliness, desperation, anguish, and finally alienation, with the ultimate realization that he alone is responsible for the answers to his problems. Certain events (e.g., death, suffering, guilt) provide the opportunity for a more transcendental decision; these are called "limit-situations." Such decisions mark the difference between existence and essence, or the desire for authenticity and self-definition. One defines one's essence through the act of conscious choice and the assumption of responsibility for one's actions.

Many of these ideas are evident in *tremendista* works, but to state that the novels themselves are philosophical works would be stretching the point. Similarities are evident, particularly in the characters' existential anguish and the question of free will, but *tremendismo* tends to the aesthetic interpretation rather than the elaboration of an ontological position.[6] Further, it is impossible to ascertain whether there was a direct influence of existential philosophers on Spanish writers or whether the novelists were simply echoing an international or generational concern for the plight of man in modern society. The question is further complicated in this instance because, as one philosopher remarked, many components of existentialism have been part of Spanish thought for centuries.[7] Finally, the *tremendista* novel is a more intuitive, less intellectually structured work, and as such does not seek to provide a literary vehicle for a philosophical system, as do some of Sartre's plays and novels, for example.

La familia de Pascual Duarte

Camilo José Cela has consistently been at the forefront of new movements in the contemporary Spanish novel since the 1940s, particularly in the cultivation of form as an expression of idea. His experimentation with *tremendismo* offered a new path for the novel and seemed to reflect the contemporary spirit of the Spanish people ideologically and aesthetically. The reality of the postwar situation, with its memory of recent cruelty, deprivation, misery, and the questions of future possibilities, seems to take shape symbolically in *La familia de Pascual Duarte*. In his memoirs, the condemned criminal tries to justify his life by presenting the circumstances that led to his present situation (a procedure recalling the picaresque mode both in the "moral" tone and in the episodic nature of the work). His remarks are interspersed with editorial comments, letters, or postscripts by various individuals and the person who "found" the manuscript, a technique that offers multiple perspectives on the story.

The opening sentence sets the tone for the reader: "I, sir, am not mad, although I wouldn't lack reasons for being so."[8] With these words, Pascual begins the account of his unhappy life. His existence is filled with misery and violence: his mother was cruel and ill-natured, his father died a ghastly death of rabies, his retarded brother had his ears chewed off by a pig and later drowned in a barrel of oil, his sister became a prostitute and was the lover of his enemy El Estirao, his first wife was unfaithful to him with the same El Estirao, his two children died. Yet Pascual's characterization of himself as a rather sensitive, resigned victim contrasts sharply with the violent deeds he commits: he rapes his fiancée, knifes a man, and kills his dog, his mare, his first wife and her lover, his mother, and the Count of Torremejía.

The novel progresses in the interplay among three levels of relationships. The social perspective provides a contextual framework, but although society determined Pascual's crime and punishment, it is the least important factor. On another level, the novel depicts Pascual's contact with people outside his immediate family who undermine the family honor or the integrity of his person (e.g., El Estirao). The point at which the social world intersects with his family life is of great consequence, since it is both cause and determinant of his action. The third and deepest level, the epicenter of the work, completely separated from any outside factors, is his relationship with his mother. It differs from the other levels because (1) it is a constant factor throughout his life, (2) the murder of his mother is premeditated, and (3) he explains and analyzes his attitude and growing hatred in a more lucid fashion. Each level of relationships complements the others, and is selected because it sheds light on the violent behavior that characterizes his life.

The arrangement of narrative voices provides a stylistic reflection of the relationships described above, paralleling the tension created by inner and outer forces.[9] In order of appearance the sources are (1) the transcriber's note, (2) the letter to don Joaquín (a friend of the man Pascual murdered) from Pascual Duarte, (3) a portion of don Joaquín's will, (4) the dedication of Pascual Duarte's memoirs, and (5) the memoirs themselves, finished by (6) another note from the transcriber and comments on Pascual's last moments by (7) a priest and (8) a guard at the jail. The additional information added to Pascual's narrative is often contradictory or designed to make the reader note discrepancies in fact or chronology.

Throughout the memoirs, Pascual makes constant mention of external causes for the violent direction that his life has taken in an effort to remove from his shoulders some of the responsibility for his actions. The most apparent are the numerous references to fate, destiny, predestination, and so on; for example: "Whoever destiny pursues will never free himself even though he hides under stones" (27). The theme of fate is also stylistically reinforced through metaphor, image, or allusion ("The days went by one the same as the other . . . with the same presentiments of a storm clouding our vision" [119]).

These constant references to fate also help to remove the novel from its specific social setting to an atemporal, mythic plane where behavioral codes are less conditioned by time and culture. Pascual cannot escape his bad luck, notes one critic.[10] Yet, from the reader's limited point of view, this bad luck may be the result of Pascual's tragic flaw, blindness to contemporary behavioral codes. His reactions are not those of a person who is integrated into a modern society, whose laws depersonalize crime and vengeance, placing retribution under the aegis of a legal system. On the contrary, the code used throughout *La familia* is a more primitive one: with the exception of the mother's death, each crime is instinctual, immediate, and directly related to vengeance or personal honor (only the circumstances surrounding the Count's death are never explained). On this level, abstract ideas of right and wrong, good and evil, do not count as much as the personal value system that determines Pascual's actions.

An equally good case, however, could be made for Pascual as a contemporary Everyman. His feeling of strangeness in relation to others and his need to take definitive action to prove that he is authentic place him in the line of the modern existential hero, whose apparently gratuitous actions are in effect a type of self-definition. The solitude and alienation of the typical existential character are also present in Pascual and determine his feeling of exclusion. Several points have been made connecting *La familia* with the existential movement and even certain similarities have been established with Camus's *The Stranger,* published in the same year.[11]

Cela's manipulation of the grotesque creates a tension that complements the constant physical and mental violence. Incongruity in the inversion of emotional values increases narrative tension: the association of laughter with unhappiness, for example. His mother laughs at the terrible suffering of her husband and when her lover kicks her son; Lola smiles only after Pascual rapes her or when he accidentally runs into an old lady. This inferred violence is furthered by numerous references to blood and the use of negative nature or animal motifs (e.g., the metaphorical "thorn" in his side; images of cut flowers, which die; the mother's eyes, associated with those of a snake). Finally, the tenderness with which he describes certain events or points of view is out of character considering the violent circumstances (e.g., the bowtie they put on his dead brother seems like "a butterfly that, in its innocence, happened to light on a corpse" [38]); certain poetic devices of repetition, motif, and so forth contrast with the unsavory events. Thus incongruity creates a deliberate stylistic tension between the facts (including violence and hatred) and the method with which they are related.

Finally, the novelistic procedure of supplementing Pascual's account with those of other people, presenting contradictory facts, and casting doubt on the veracity of the memoirs, raises questions concerning the entire manuscript, the narrative, and even Pascual's attitude. Certain elements greatly increase the ambiguity surrounding the events: the extreme selectiveness of the memoirs, the question as to just how much "editing" the transcriber performed. The transcriber discovers chronological conflicts (revealed by the color of the ink with which Pascual wrote a letter and two chapters) suggesting that "our character was not as forgetful or confused as he would seem at first glance" (125). The mystery surrounding the death of the Count and the conflicting descriptions of Pascual's last moments in the two postscripts end the novel with questions rather than answers. The intimation that Pascual went to his death a coward rather than with manly stoicism, as Pascual would have the reader believe, shakes the reader's confidence in Pascual's good faith. This technique implies a greater participation of the reader, who must decide where the truth really lies. One critic offers a further thought on ambiguity and reader participation: the unexplained editing and contradictory information allow the reader to participate indirectly in the feeling of arbitrary censorship and moral contradictions prevalent in the early postwar period.[12]

Although *tremendismo* may have been latent in Spanish literature before this time, *La familia de Pascual Duarte* gave a new energy to the realism of the 1940s with its experimentation, the creation of mood, the exclusion of sequential facts, emphasis on the untypical individual, the movement away from the bourgeois class (either as object of criticism or as the main character), the addition of a mythic overlay, the strange juxtaposition of violence with lyricism, and the almost playful attitude of the text in the contradictory narrative voices (e.g., the dedication, the preliminary letters)—all techniques that become common only some twenty years later when traditional and social realism give way to a less documentary approach to reality.

Nada

The innovational subject matter of *Nada* (1944) was not the only reason for the popularity of this first Nadal prize-winner. Carmen Laforet was a young woman, and completely unknown in literary circles, an unusual combination that piqued the curiosity of the reading public. *Nada* displays a greater social orientation than does *La familia de Pascual Duarte* because of its firm establishment within a definite time and place.

The novel opens as Andrea arrives in Barcelona after the war to study at the university. She lives with relatives in crowded, filthy surroundings, and the tensions created by their unpleasant relationships make her life unbearable. Andrea's experiences are framed by two antithetical situations: the desirable, "normal" world of her fellow students and her attraction to the possibilities that they represent versus the sordid, petty, often grotesque atmosphere of the apartment on Aribau Street. For a time, the two worlds merge when her friend Ena begins to visit Andrea's sadistic, neurotic uncle Román. The visits prove to be Ena's scheme to avenge her mother, jilted by Román many years ago, and Román's suicide dramatically and symbolically closes the chapter in their life. Andrea decides for the hope of the future and leaves one day at dawn for Madrid, a job, and a new life. Constant themes of hunger, poverty, dirt, unhappiness, and disillusion underline the plot.

Unlike *La familia de Pascual Duarte,* whose plot involved Pascual's contact with a small number of people, *Nada* concentrates on shifting group dynamics for its development. Of the several clearly separated groups, the family on Aribau Street offers the best examples of the use of personal relationships to move the plot and determine the overall atmosphere of the novel. The grandmother is senile; Andrea's uncle Juan and Gloria have constant marital fights; Aunt Angustias rigidly oversees the family honor (she eventually joins a convent after an implied affair with her employer, a former suitor); Uncle Román, increasingly deranged, enjoys setting one member against another. Finally, the silent, hostile vigilance of the maid completes the picture.

The story is revealed through these family scenes as Andrea describes them, and many of them are extremely unpleasant: screams, hysterics, constant arguments, spying, insinuations, and even physical violence form part of their everyday life. Each scene intentionally introduces a note of mystery, suspense, or surprise. Yet of greater consequence is the creation of the atmosphere that such interaction produces, since the entire family lives in a constant state of tension. Further, each family member provides a norm against which Andrea measures her own development. Angustias and Gloria offer antithetical role models (the rigid spinster versus the animal-like, sensual woman) both of which are rejected; for Andrea as a woman, the two brothers (Juan and Román) incarnate all the potentials for unhappiness with self and with others.

The psychological state of the family is faithfully reflected in their apartment; dust, filth, disorder, and accumulation of useless or unused possessions are symbolic of the inability to clear away the cobwebs of past family relationships. Even the more neutral descriptions convey the suffocating oppression of objects and are symbolic of Andrea's own restrictions and lack of independence. Other passages are indicative of Andrea's state of mind; their metaphoric dimensions reinforce her negative feelings of unhappiness and tension. For example, her observations of the bathroom convey the feeling of trapped desperation that gives *Nada* much of its *tremendista* quality: "That bathroom seemed like a witches' house. The dirty walls preserved marks of clawed hands, of cries of desperation. Everywhere the chipped walls opened their toothless mouths oozing with moisture. . . . Madness grimaced in the twisted faucets."[13] Ordinary objects are charged with negative emotional values and the reader perceives Andrea's own anxiety through the reaction to objects that suddenly become menacing in their unfamiliarity.

Nada and Cela's *La familia* are both concerned with a psychological state of mind rather than exterior descriptions. Both trace the desire of the character to come to terms with himself, define himself, and shape his life around some goal or meaning—a desire that transcends the action per se. The narrative structure also offers some similarities. Both employ the device of presenting reminiscences. The split between narrator and character (the older Andrea writing about the younger one's experiences) colors the tone of the novel and creates a temporal separation between the two. The narrator controls the limited information accessible to the reader, which also allows more freedom for commentary and justifies distortion and selectivity.

Foreboding and reference to fate or destiny are present in *Nada* in much the same manner as in *La familia de Pascual Duarte*—that is, much of the blame for tragic or unhappy events is attributed to an outside source. Andrea's solitude is "something that seemed unavoidable" (152); the unpleasantness that often follows a happy period in her life is "a fatal law" (75); she feels trapped by cosmic forces (229) and finally decides that one might as well let matters run their course without trying to interfere or change them (215, 229).

As in *La familia,* there is a certain amount of ambiguity surrounding the situation in *Nada.* Since the novelistic perspective is limited strictly to immediate perceptions with little background or history, there is a lack of psychological definition of the other characters, except for external evidence and remarks by the narrator. Thus there is a constant shifting of opinion as an apparently contradictory mode of behavior suddenly becomes clear with the appearance of new evidence. In the words of the grandmother, "Not everything is what it seems to be" (83), a remark that has wider implications than the specific situation to which she refers. The narrator even makes the "happy ending" of the novel somewhat ambiguous: Andrea leaves Barcelona for a new life, remarking that she took nothing from the Aribau house with her. She then contradicts herself, observing, "At least, that's what I thought at the time" (300), clearly implying that all was not resolved by the escape from her relatives. The relativity of truth also contributes to undermining conventional behavioral patterns. The positive values against which one would normally measure behavior are missing. These experiences contribute to Andrea's sense of disillusionment, which is an important theme. The naive optimism with which she begins her stay soon turns to dismay as she learns that life is not a fairy tale, that she is being used by friends and relatives alike, that reality goes beyond surface appearance.

The specific spatiotemporal framework of *Nada* leads to an easier identification of this novel with a national situation. The atmosphere of despair, hopelessness, anxiety, and hunger pervading the book reflects the postwar circumstances of physical and mental misery. The characters could well represent various aspects of Spanish life and culture of the early postwar days: the two brothers who fought on opposite sides of the Civil War, the senile grandmother as the powerless older generation, the effete Bohemians who reject their parents' middle-class values, the more serious students. Andrea must abandon the past in order to begin a new life, and in this interpretation, her departure is not so much an escape as a conscious choice for liberty and self-sufficiency.

On a more universal plane, the novel can be seen as a chronicle of the maturation of an adolescent girl into the role of adult, with its concomitant responsibilities and assimilation of social codes. There are decided rites of passage she must undergo and a series of "tests" that she takes in her growth. Her dreams of romantic life are shattered in a parody of the Cinderella story, when she attends a party at Pons's house. She rejects the role models offered to her (Gloria and Angustias) and opts for a different path. The conflict between generations in this case represents the discarding of old values for new ones. [14]

As a *tremendista* novel, *Nada* lacks the emphatic violence of Cela's work. Instead, there is an insistent accumulation of sordid, unpleasant details that unite to create a bleak picture. References to the nightmare aspects of Andrea's existence, the unhappiness, the perverted relationships described above, the revolting details ("from the dust-laden corners and grimy wallpaper a flock of hungry bed bugs began to emerge" [200]), cruelty, lack of communication, the erratic behavior of the family, the shabby everyday reality, form a nagging background of unpleasantness.

A case for connections between Laforet's *tremendismo* and existentialism can be made, with conclusions similar to those for Cela's *La familia:* namely, that direct influence is unlikely, but the spirit of the philosophical tenets is present, if only intuitively. Whereas the characters of Camus and Cela seem to show a certain kinship, in *Nada* Laforet comes closer to Sartre's literary interpretation of existential action, as seen in *La nausée (Nausea,* 1938). Certain intriguing points of contact emerge: the general feelings of anxiety and loss of control, symbolized in the awareness of material objects— "things"—that seem to have a life of their own, menacing the protagonist; and the potentially redemptive power of art in life (such as Román's music, Andrea's own writing). Sartre's character is more analytically aware of a crisis of existence, brought to a head by his realization of the existence of inanimate objects, but the feelings of unease and anxiety, the accumulation of unpleasant or unusual episodes that reinforce the idea of the absurdity of existence, are present in *Nada*. Andrea's final decision to leave, interpreted as her symbolic choice for independence, may imply the philosophical idea of choice as freedom.

If considered as a discrete literary movement, *tremendismo* was confined to few writers. As a variant of realism, however, it is long-lived in the sense that many novelists have freely used its aesthetic of truculence for their specific and often varying purposes. The conscious incorporation of select characteristics of *tremendismo* has become a common practice following Cela and Laforet. Cela himself has continued to use accumulated elements of violence and anguish in most of his later works; Laforet's subsequent books also follow the direction of *Nada*. Many Civil War narratives describe gory scenes of destruction or stress the misery and disorientation both of the soldiers and of the citizens or the consequences of the holocaust. Fernández de la Reguera's *Cuando voy a morir* (When I Die, published as *In the Darkness of my Fury,* 1950), José Luis Castillo-Puche's *El vengador* (The avenger, 1956) and Ana María Matute's *Los hijos muertos*

(Dead children, published as *The Lost Children*, 1958) are examples of this. A host of lesser figures are also associated with the excesses of *tremendismo*, including Rafael García Serrano (b. 1917) and Tomás Borrás (b. 1891). *Tremendista* elements often enhance feelings of loneliness, despair, anguish, and alienation—attitudes common to the works of subjective realists such as Matute, or novels describing death obsessions—Miguel Delibes's *La sombra del ciprés es alargada* (Long is the cypress's shadow, 1948) or Castillo-Puche's *Con la muerte al hombro* (With death at my shoulder, 1954).

Although the early examples of *tremendismo* did not take a clearly critical stance on specific social issues, later adaptations have used their techniques to illustrate an exposé of social evils or human cruelty. *Tremendismo*—the concentration on less agreeable aspects of reality—is a fresh interpretation of what critics have signaled as the "unbroken" line of realism in Spain.

Chapter Four
Neorealism:
Three Interpretations

Traditional realism was a continuation of an accepted literary tradition; *tremendismo*—a distortion of basic reality—was the hallmark of a small number of writers and was adapted in limited measure to suit the varying purposes of later novelists. Both movements are associated with the 1940s and 1950s, although they continue to this day. Realism also characterizes the 1950s and 1960s, the years in which the Spanish novel became more cohesive in ideology and form. The focus shifts, however, to a critical interpretation that betrays a greater commitment to nonaesthetic concerns. Neorealism is the general name applied to the postwar version, distinguishing it from earlier movements.

A new group of writers emerged in the 1950s, with enough common background and literary interest to be called the Generation of 1954 or the *Generación de medio siglo* (The Mid-Century Generation), so named because the first work by several of the constituents appeared in this year. These people were united by approximate age (born between 1925 and 1935), by the fact that they had experienced the Civil War as children (perhaps one of the reasons that few write "war novels," although the Civil War forms an obsessive leitmotif in their works), and by their common critical stance concerning contemporary Spanish reality.[1] The critical attitude that characterizes their works may be historically or socially oriented, or more generally diffused in a sense of nonconformity with contemporary values (particularly those incarnated by the bourgeoisie) and a feeling of solidarity with all those who suffer, in sentiments of alienation with contemporary conditions and culture, and in a radical break with the historical continuum expressed in an Adanic attitude, which reveals their feeling that they are not responsible for past history.[2] One critic states that these writers were united in their understanding of the literary phenomenon as the expression of the social and ethical behavior of the individual.[3]

Juan Goytisolo characterizes the members of the Mid-Century Generation through their reaction against social, political, religious, and moral conformity, characteristic of the literature of the period, and one critic adds to their nonconformist attitude their hope for constructive change.[4] In even more general terms, each of these novelists practiced a literature of commitment, although their aims and the cause they served varied from a personal or existential position to a more obviously social objective. One of the authors of this generation explains that literature must shake the reader from his complacent situation: "The novel . . . must wound . . . the consciousness of society, in a desire to improve it,"[5] a telling statement that suggests the direct impact art is to have on extraliterary factors.

Novelists associated with this generation include Ignacio Aldecoa (1924–1969), Armando López Salinas (b. 1925), Carmen Martín Gaite (1925), Antonio Ferres (1925), Jesús Fernández Santos (1926), Ana María Matute (1926), José Manuel Caballero Bonald (1926), Rafael Sánchez Ferlosio (1927), Juan García Hortelano (1928), Alfonso Grosso (1928), Juan Goytisolo (1931), Daniel Sueiro (1931), Juan Marsé (1933), and Luis Goytisolo Gay (1935). Two geographical groupings—Madrid and Barcelona—and two publications (*Revista española* and *Laye*) offer further evidence of affiliation.[6] This list could be considerably expanded with the addition of writers cultivating other genres or with those sharing common literary interests who extend the chronological limits somewhat.

Neorealism takes three directions: *objetivismo* (the elimination of the authorial point of view and an expositional approach); the social novel, which uses an extensively descriptive, documentary literature to reveal problems in specific social and economic sectors of contemporary Spain; and subjective realism, an extremely personal interpretation of the same problems, which employs many of the literary devices that the first two movements prefer to ignore. All three modes overlap chronologically and it is not uncommon to note characteristics of one appearing in the other. However, the major differences can be understood in the divergence between a dogmatically committed approach to art (the ideological taking precedence over other considerations) and the introduction of an aesthetic overlay that may soften the direct impact of the possible social criticism.

The choice of realism as the most appropriate means of presentation during this period can be attributed to political as well as artistic causes. Censorship had closely watched the media's treatment of matters dealing with the Franco regime, and unfavorable criticism of issues related to contemporary reality—social, economic, religious, and political criticism—was forbidden. Since such material could not appear in newspapers, writers of fiction consequently took upon themselves the task traditionally relegated to the journalists. In the words of one of these novelists: "Spanish novelists—because of the fact that their public does not have at its disposal reliable means of information with respect to the problems that their country confronts—answer their readers' need by tracing the fairest and most equitable picture possible of the reality that they see. In this way, the novel fulfills a testimonial function in Spain that corresponds to the press in France and in the rest of Europe. . . ."[7] This statement explains the reasons underlying the "objective" position of the novelist; documentary presentation or reportage also suggests a contrivedly neutral position with regard to inflammatory statements or critical perspectives which censorship policy would have prohibited otherwise. While the regime constructed a myth of national well-being and in its propaganda depicted an era of plenitude undisturbed by historical circumstance, the neorealists severely contradicted this idyllic picture: "In the decade of the 50s it was sufficient to describe reality. Presenting its forms of appearance, they sketched a contrast with the idealized version and fulfilled a cognitive function as well as a task that was socially necessary."[8]

The collective impact of the Generation of 1898 was not felt substantially by the neorealists (except in specific cases).[9] But Baroja's realistic depiction of Spain's early twentieth century was similar to the documentary approach of the young writers. Closer to their own generation is Camilo José Cela, whose open-ended concept of the novel, choice of multiple characters of humble or middle-class provenance, and use of popular language may well have provided considerable inspiration for the social novelists. National literature, both classical and modern, was more easily available during the formative period of these writers. Time and again both authors and critics emphasize the lack of contact with international currents.

As the regime felt more secure, it relaxed its restrictive policies and allowed foreign cultural influences to penetrate Spanish life. The younger novelists became acquainted with Italian neorealism and were particularly impressed with the documentary approach to social problems, a technique adapted from the cinema as well as from the earlier novel. The subject matter of the 1950 Italian cinema revealed a kinship of interests: everyday reality presented in documentarylike fashion was particularly predominant in the Italian neorealist cinema. Dating from approximately 1945–51, associated with directors Roberto Rossellini, Vittorio DeSica and Luchino Visconti, it emphasized gray existence, stark misery with no mitigating fantastic or escapist themes. The year 1950 marked the introduction of Italian neorealism in Spain, by means of the "Italian Cinema Week."

The interest in objective presentation, reproduction of everyday life and speech, and the attention to social structures also appear in Italian neorealistic fiction at this time. Cesare Pavese, Elio Vittorini, Italo Calvino, Vasco Pratolini, Carlo Levi, and Alberto Moravia are among the most influential of the Italian novelists, and their writings affected the more critical Spanish social neorealists. Cesare Zavattine, one of the theoreticians of the movement, was translated by Rafael Sánchez Ferlosio, a leader of Spanish objectivism. [10]

Many aspects of European literature and thought find echoes in neorealism. The most persistent foreign influence has come from France: Proust and Bergson; existential literature, particularly that by Sartre and Camus; the French New Novel (Alain Robbe-Grillet, Nathalie Sarraute, Michel Butor, Marguerite Duras, etc.). More experimental Spaniards turn to Kafka, Beckett, and especially James Joyce for a number of innovative techniques. Of course, the presence of any number of other writers and philosophers can be traced in individual cases.

The American novelists of the period, particularly the "Lost Generation," were avidly read in translation: the Spaniards recognize John Dos Passos, Erskine Caldwell, John Steinbeck, Ernest Hemingway, and William Faulkner, collectively and individually, as fascinating innovators. Their technique was characterized by external, impassive descriptions reflecting inner moods. Of special interest to the objectivists was Dos Passos's use of social themes, the "Camera Eye," and the unanimist techniques of *Manhattan Transfer* (1925).

Giving further cohesion to the movement were two intellectuals whose theoretical studies of objective realism gave form and direction to its development in Spain. José María Castellet, a respected Catalan critic, already well known for his interest in existential and sociological criticism, wrote *La hora del lector* (The reader's time, 1957), [11] in which he traces the declining role of the narrator from the bourgeois literature of the nineteenth century to the modern novel. Viewing the objective novel as distinctly antibourgeois (a stance taken by many of the writers themselves), he suggests that this technique marks the abandonment of the safe, orderly world of the middle class, displaying in its stead individual instability and solitude. Aesthetically, the "reader's time" is his growing participation in the novel because of this technique; reading becomes a creative art.

Juan Goytisolo published *Problemas de la novela* in 1959 as a defense against the attacks aimed at recent novels that followed the dictates of social and objectivist norms. "Today," he stated, "the word psychology is one of those words that no conscientious author can pronounce without blushing."[12] He discusses how the novelist's awareness of his lack of omniscience has given rise to a procedure that shows that there are no longer any absolute truths, only relativism and ambiguity. His 1959 article "Para una literatura nacional" (For a national literature) began a literary polemic concerning the purpose and execution of a literary work.[13]

Aesthetically, Goytisolo and Castellet agree completely with the philosophical tenets of objectivism, and as well with the aesthetic concerns used to achieve them. There is, however, a serious divergence between Spanish objectivism and the international (i.e., French) branch representing the new movement. The Spanish neorealists never abandoned their conception of literature as means to an end: the social content was never completely ignored. This position was confirmed in an International Colloquium on the Novel held at Formentor in 1959, where the two divergent interpretations became clear. Robbe-Grillet attended and expressed his opinion that the novel was an end in itself, with no transcendental value save as a work of art. Both Castellet and Goytisolo responded to this point of view in their theoretical works, clearly stating that literature demands of the writer both social responsibility and a commitment to his society and his time.[14] In theory, both critics were correct in their assessment of the writers' interest in literature of commitment. Each variant of neorealism, however, selects different technical means of conveying a critical attitude to the reader, as will be seen in the following chapters.

Chapter Five
Objetivismo

Objetivismo ("objectivism") is the natural consequence of the stance adopted by neorealism, which makes the author a witness rather than a creator, an informer rather than a judge. The objectivist novel proceeds to eliminate authorial intrusion and present only perceptible reality from which the reader must gather and sort out the elements he deems most important. Only surface phenomena are present, and any psychological content not directly observable (e.g., tears as an indication of unhappiness) is eliminated.

Influences that affected this movement were not only literary. Behaviorism, a branch of psychology that maintains that only observable behavior can give clues to the subject's inner makeup, offers the same perspective as that of objectivism. The impact of phenomenology on twentieth-century Western philosophy may have affected neorealism, too, although—to judge from the absence of direct acknowledgment of firsthand acquaintance with the theories—the influence was indirect. Phenomenology, which has so radically changed the outlook of contemporary philosophy, reduces essence to pure experience. Husserl, Scheler, and Merleau-Ponty develop ideas that have close affinities with Spanish modes of thought. Merleau-Ponty's existentialist phenomenology coincides with several of the objectivist theoretical practices (particularly in his analysis of behavior, perception, and time); and Scheler's interpretation of phenomenology was studied at some length in the prewar issues of the *Revista de Occidente*.[1]

The most significant literary inspiration of objectivism can be traced to the French *nouveau roman* ("new novel"), a phenomenon of the 1950s and 1960s, whose writers reacted against traditional literary conventions of the realistic novel with its linear plot, psychological development, and particularly its omniscient author. This does not preclude inclusion of the psychological state of the character, but rather those devices that convey it: transmittal of background, relationships, and the usual commentaries on the reactions and emotions arising from given situations. The story evolves in a continual present tense, in which perceptions that register on the character are communicated without evaluative judgment. Alain Robbe-Grillet's early novels provide objective, detailed visual descriptions. Nathalie Sarraute's interest turns more toward dialogue, which in her opinion reveals the "subconversational world" of the speakers. Other authors such as Claude Simon or Michel Butor develop their particular theories, but all react in their own way against literary convention typified by the omniscient author.[2]

The possibilities offered by the cinema also exerted a telling influence on the neorealists, and in particular on the objectivists. The "impartiality" of the camera eye was attractive to the writers: it allows the visual scene to make the impact, using artistic technique rather than interpolations, and permits the viewer to make the judgment. Other techniques, such as collage and montage, sequencing, close-ups, slow motion, were transferred to the printed page.[3] One writer of the movement states, "In my novels, people move cinematographically, I almost move the camera, including when I am narrating inner processes. . . ."[4]

Since neither plot line nor character analysis directs the movement of the novel, certain structural intricacies must take their place. While not completely excluding the idea of a "main" character, the objectivist writers tend to work with large numbers of people, either one by one in a number of mini-episodes or, more importantly, in group interaction. Thus the novel moves from the single protagonist, or main character, to the "multiple protagonist," a feature that both serves the author's distrust of psychological interiorization and allows a certain social stance in the identification of these people with representative groups.[5] In general, no single character enjoys prime importance. Instead, group interaction allows for a confrontation of dissimilar types: bourgeois/lower class, younger/older, city/country, rich/poor. The dialectic created smacks as much of the sociological as of the social, as the typology of the group becomes clear through their behavior.

Superficial values, egotism, selfishness, boredom, vacuousness, and alienation are portrayed as characteristics of bourgeois life. Juan Goytisolo's *La isla* (The island, published as *The Sands of Torremolinos,* 1961), chronicles the unhappiness of this directionless kind of existence. Juan García Hortelano's *Tormenta de verano* (*Summer Storm,* 1961) describes a brief period in a town of wealthy summer vacationers: the discovery of a dead body and subsequent investigations parallel the troubles of an alienated individual who finally opts for conformism; his *Nuevas amistades* (New friendships, 1959) is another version of life among the younger bourgeois set: drinking and parties are the main pastimes in their empty existence, structured momentarily by an unwanted—and false—pregnancy. Luis Goytisolo's *Las mismas palabras* (The same words, 1962) deals with the same type of boredom, set in the dolce vita context of Barcelona youth. The monotony and pettiness of life in a provincial town appear in Carmen Martín Gaite's *Entre visillos* (Behind curtains, 1958). In an extreme example of this technique, Jorge Trulock's *Inventorio base* (Base inventory, 1969) follows the lives of an ordinary family, merging conversation, activities, and author's words to create a close-up view of conversations and objects. Some of these works present sensitive, rebellious individuals who express dissatisfaction with the status quo, a desire for a purpose in life or for commitment to a cause or idea, reminiscent of some of the literature of the American Lost Generation. Their fate is ultimate failure or the realization that it is impossible to fight the system.

Those novelists who espouse the techniques of objectivism never deny their interest in the social content of their works. Interviews, colloquia, and articles reveal their opinion that a social consciousness should form at least a minimal part of the writer's literary creed.[6] In a backward glance at this movement, García Hortelano states that "objective realism was the name of what a few of us practiced, a type of French . . . objectivism à la Robbe Grillet. . . . But that realism did not claim to be objective . . . but rather critical and social."[7]

In fact, most objectivist novels disclose the author's presence through techniques other than direct intervention, perhaps as a compromise between the demands of aesthetics and those of ideology. The selection of raw material betrays the author's social concerns; the arrangement of that material is the commentary on it, and places the novelist in a position similar to that of the movie director, in his manipulation of elements through montage, collage, superimposition, or juxtaposition. In the best objectivist novels, this technique is raised to a very sophisticated level.

Spatial and temporal loci suffer drastic reduction in scope, suggesting a classical unity of time and place. Severely restricted to a continual present because of the distrust of interior flashback, objectivism eliminates all remembrances except those communicated in speech. Thus they reject possibilities of enriching the content with material from the past. Further, the novel takes place within a limited physical area (Madrid and environs, a vacation resort, a river beach). The technique of placing a large number of characters within such limits is called *unanimismo* and influenced Spanish writers through French sources and the American writer Dos Passos.

Since the author presents surface reality in a manner that can only be apprehended empirically, it stands to reason that the obvious vehicles to transmit this information are sight and sound. Objective descriptions skim the surface, capturing distance, color, spatial relationships, but in the most orthodox novels never direct the reader toward a specific evaluation. A major emphasis is placed on knowledge gleaned from "overhearing" the characters' conversations. As discourse gains greater preeminence, the accurate transmittal of dialogue or speech is raised to a fine art, developed and carefully elaborated as the most apt vehicle to convey the type, class, and thoughts of the protagonist. Conversations on inane subjects or matters of everyday life shape the direction of the book. The reproduction of dialogue is the single characteristic that most distinguishes the objectivist novel. Gone are the elegant turn of phrase, the metaphor, the careful balance of style. In their place the writer provides banal, trite, everyday reality, replete with unfinished sentences, interjections, often extremely trivial subject matter. In fact, many critics praise the skill with which the novelists manage to convey the characters' speech, while at the same time bemoaning the artistic and thematic limitations caused by such accuracy.

A hoped-for result of external fidelity in reproducing conversations is the "objectivity" in revealing the characters' inner thoughts. The introduction of the interior monologue allows self-presentation without the necessity of an intermediary. The perspective is still limited to the individual concerned, with no commentary on the author's part to provide the reader with any privileged information with which to understand or analyze the character. According to Castellet, the introduction of the interior monologue signals the abandonment of a sense of security and order associated with bourgeois life, substituted at this point with instability and individual solitude.

Optimally, the technical characteristics of the objectivist novel allow the material to present itself without authorial interference (as suggested by the various names applied to the movement—behaviorism, conductism, *novela de la mirada* ["visual novel"]).

However, it would be difficult if not impossible to adhere to the theoretical suggestions completely in practice. Even with the elimination of direct commentary, intervention, descriptions, or traditional rhetorical devices, the mere selection and arrangement of material would involve a certain amount of authorial "participation." Parallels can be drawn from structural arrangement; by the very deemphasis of description, what is provided will stand out all the more in significance. Objectivism was cultivated in its pure form by only a few writers. Some authors inject their obvious presence; others use a more documentary or testimonial approach, emphasizing in this way a more evident social concern. However, the novelists' control over the text was discarded by many and in its place they adopted the technique of unanimism (of the multiple character) and the objectivist point of view. The originality of objectivism was touted, its excesses severely criticized;[8] besides the introduction of the new perspective, this movement was instrumental in adding a distinctly aesthetic dimension to the tradition of Spanish realism.

Although many works fall under the general heading of objectivism, three outstanding novels, each representing a different interpretation of the theoretical bases, are indicative of the ways in which objectivism was interpreted in Spain. Camilo José Cela's *La colmena* (*The Hive*) represents an early experiment with point of view and unanimism; *Los bravos* (The untamed) uses objectivist techniques to describe collective protagonists in a rural setting; Rafael Sánchez Ferlosio's *El Jarama* is a tightly woven masterpiece exposing a cross-section of Spanish population through dialogue and interaction.

La colmena

La colmena (*The Hive*), one of the first conscious efforts at experimentation with techniques associated with objectivism, was written substantially earlier than the dates associated with the movement. Cela was not even part of the generation most associated with neorealism: he began the novel in 1945 and, after some problems with censorship, had it published in Argentina in 1951.[9]

Although this novel does not conform wholly with the techniques of the objectivist writers, it shares enough characteristics to be placed in this category: the one obvious difference is the authorial presence, which intrudes in a number of ways. Despite some initial adverse reactions (according to Cela, he was expelled from the Press Association and his name was not allowed to be mentioned in the press), critics and public soon realized that Cela had managed to produce another landmark and acknowledged its importance in the history of the Spanish novel as well as its intrinsic value. [10]

The subject matter of *La colmena* was not startlingly new: Madrid, the years of hunger following the Civil War, man's inhumanity to man, exploitation, disgusting or pathetic descriptions, emotional and physical violence—these were elements that could be found in greater or lesser combination in any number of novels of the period. However, the structural form of *La colmena* recombined and amalgamated a series of partial visions of reality into an overwhelming totality. The technique, untried in Spanish literature to this point, suggested new possibilities in elasticity of novelistic form. [11]

The most notable feature of *La colmena* is its fragmentary nature, which effectively destroys traditional notions of cause and effect, breaks down linear time, and avoids psychological development. In the place of these literary conventions, Cela offers brief glimpses of over one hundred characters—depending on the source, they range from a low of 160 (Cela) to 346 (Caballero Bonald)[12]—loosely connected by physical coincidence in certain locales (a café, an apartment house), by acquaintance, or by family ties. The three-day time span is broken into small sections ranging from one paragraph to several pages. Kaleidoscopic shifts among characters and scenes blur the sequence, suggesting a continual present tense without the continuity of past or future. The large number of characters shifts the focus from individual development to relationships and interaction.

The two "main characters" (main by virtue of the fact that they appear more than others) represent the two extremes of the social scale—exploiter and victim. Doña Rosa, the "Queen bee" and owner of the café that is one of the gathering places, is presented in less than flattering terms: "[She smiles] at her clients, whom she hates deep down, with her little blackened teeth, full of filth" (22). She is cruel to subordinates, insensitive to others (at one point she delivers a disquisition on overeating and intestinal problems to a starving prostitute); she delights in humiliating and berating her employees.

Martín Marco, the victim, provides another tenuous thread of continuity in *La colmena*. An unemployed writer, he lives from hand to mouth, mainly on the charity of his sister, much to the chagrin of her resentful husband. In the course of the novel, Martín is tossed out of doña Rosa's café for not paying, visits his sister, encounters various friends who give him money or buy him food and drink, spends the night in a house of prostitution, makes a pilgrimage to his mother's grave in the outskirts of the city, then walks back toward Madrid from the cemetery, under his arm an unopened newspaper that contains some damaging information concerning him, the contents of which are never disclosed. Other characters include young Victoria, who sells herself in order to get money to buy her tubercular boyfriend the necessary medicine; the homosexual Suárez, whose aged mother had been found murdered earlier in the day (he spends an evening with a friend and is arrested without being informed of the reason); the pathetic aging prostitute Elvira, and don Roque's family, whose ostensibly moral and religious tenets contrast with the fact that both daughter and father are having clandestine affairs.

The extensive number of actions or characters presented in a reduced space and time conforms with the unanimist method, introduced by Cela in such a way that *La colmena* was dubbed the "most valuable and significant novel published in Spain since 1936."[13] Cela himself commented on the unusual organization of the book, calling *La colmena* a "clock-novel," composed of "numerous wheels and little pieces, each needing the other for it to work."[14] From the point of view of the plot, such a technique provides a density of action and a concentration of vision that destroy the customary sequential narrative and force a more active role on the reader. In fact, the author himself provides the first clue to the possible approach to the work with the opening words of the novel: "Let's not lose our perspective. I'm tired of saying it, it's the only important thing," states doña Rosa to no one in particular (21). With this indirect admonition, Cela then moves on to present his episodic work, whose shifting scenes remove the reader from his privileged position of omniscient viewer.

Deprived of the conventions of character development, the reader begins to form an impression from the pattern of the episodes, seeing parallels, repetitions, uniformity of purpose. The picture that gradually develops is a grim one, revealed through the relationships among city dwellers. In general, these interactions disclose a bleak picture of human behavior: egotism, hypocrisy, lack of charity, and selfishness characterize their actions. Those who are sensitive or caring become the victims of shameless predators. The measure of success in this world is the acquisition of money, the sole factor that bestows power. This novel offers some social criticism, particularly in the rigid economic separations, the injustices, the numerous victims of the postwar situation, all of which reveal the social breakdowns of the period.[15] Political implications are also incorporated in the total picture, as seen in references to those on the losing side of the Civil War ("that disrespectful, shameless Red" [28]), who, in the opinion of many, deserve their hard lot. Cultural values also lose importance, and several intellectuals are forced to admit that their education is no longer of any usefulness.

Aside from the inverted values, numerous episodes of unwitting or deliberate cruelty suggest that human nature is basically evil. Aggressive cruelty extends even to animals: in a brief *tremendista* episode, a crowd impassively watches a dying dog's final minutes of agony as the garbage collectors toss the suffering animal into the back of their cart. Even more insidious than the overt acts is the refusal to help others. Cela comments, "People cross paths, hurriedly. No one thinks about the one next to him who unexpectedly walks along looking down at the ground, with his stomach destroyed or a cyst on one lung, or out of his head" (279).

The selfishness and egotism prevalent in these characters are enhanced by the environmental circumstance of the urban situation. Madrid, in particular, seems to embody certain evil connotations for Cela.[16] Furthermore, the traditional institutions that ideally would foster love for one's fellow man are quite noticeably missing. The Church, which could offer moral guidance or practical assistance, is represented (indirectly and ironically) by the wife of don Roque, who immerses herself in long-distance missionary work, saving the souls of Chinese children by contributing money and in turn enjoying the privilege of naming the children. She is as blind to the obvious moral problems in her own family as to the desperate plight of her neighbors.

Obsessions with sex and hunger form two interesting themes in Cela's oblique commentary in *La colmena*. Both are instincts that must be met to insure the survival of the individual or the species, a subhuman level reinforced by the numerous animal images employed in all situations.[17] Near starvation (the gypsy boy, Elvira, Martín) and constant hunger (Martín's sister, the violin player and his wife) as compared to the sumptuous meals consumed by others provide continual evidence of authorial judgment by juxtaposition or contrast. Although there are a few touching examples of conjugal love, sex is generally considered a commodity. Cela's characterization of the prostitutes shows them as victims—first of the circumstances that forced them into their profession and then of the profession itself.

A separate group is formed by mistresses of wealthy men; Cela provides an excellent sketch of a cloying girl who jealously watches over the man who keeps her. Don Roque's family offers an example of the hypocritical attitude, in the contrast between appearances and reality. Various sexual activities are represented: homosexuality, lesbianism, pedophilia, voyeurism. One particularly unsavory episode describes an older man holding the hand of a thirteen-year-old girl ("They look like an uncle who is taking his niece for a walk" [265]). Actually he is a doctor who has just bought the orphaned girl's favors from her guardian, who sends her off, saying, "Look, child, don Francisco just wants to play and besides, it has to happen someday! Don't you understand?" (265). Infrequently, the use of sex as a commodity can reveal a person's love or generosity. Victoria sells herself to buy medicine for her tubercular boyfriend. The maid who works for Martín's sister gives herself to a tavern owner to pay for the bill Martín has run up, a gratuitous act of love that is never disclosed.

Cela develops at some length the obsession with money—its accumulation, or absence; the insistence on giving the exact cost of an item no matter how insignificant (again, an "objective" way of transmitting the concerns of the characters); the immense power that it confers. The passage of time and the monotony of life are other threads woven into the fabric of the work.

Cela's participation as author differs considerably from the stance taken by the novelists of traditional realism. He exercises indirect control through the manipulation of the material itself: juxtaposition, repetition, and fragmentation are all ways in which the writer "intrudes" and makes his point. Fragmentation creates the impression of simultaneity, a synchronic rather than a diachronic view of life. Irony of circumstance, oblique commentary, and even a certain coarse humor arise from the organization of episodes. One example of juxtaposition alternates descriptions of adjoining apartments. In one room, a man is practicing a high-flown speech; in the other, a young couple discusses the bowel movements of their child: "Don Ibrahim's voice sounded solemn, like a bassoon. On the other side of the thin wall, a husband, back from his work, asked his wife 'has baby made her "poo-poo"?' " (104).

The author's opinions—"commentaries"—are evident in an enumerative technique that Cela uses sparingly for special effect. Stylistic devices in place of direct commentary preserve a measure of distance between author and reader, but Cela does not avoid deliberate intervention to convey a character's thoughts, to give a brief thumbnail sketch of circumstances or background, or even to pass judgment on the character. Don Pablo, smiling with "beatitude," comments with complete lack of understanding on the expulsion of Martín from the café: he prefers cats to humans, because they would never leave without paying. Cela adds, "If one could open his chest, one would find a heart as black and sticky as pitch" (47).

Although such examples show how Cela presents his own ideas of life through *La colmena,* he is concerned with "objectivity" in this novel, an aesthetic and ideological preoccupation that places him directly in the mainstream of neorealism. Cela himself stated that he simply reflects everyday reality, and later added that *La colmena* is a history book, not a novel.[18] The novelist is chronicler rather than creator: in Cela's words, "This novel of mine aspires only to be . . . a slice of life narrated step by step . . . exactly as life goes by" (9). Thus *La colmena* gives the impression of quick sketches with neither sequential development nor sustained commentary to aid the reader in understanding the meanings "hidden" in the actions. The overall picture arises only from the totality of the separate actions; by the same token, the "missing" moral perspective—one of the messages in the novel—can be understood only when one realizes that it is absent from the characters' behavior.

The final and most telling example of objectivity concerns the information about Martín in the newspaper. Brief episodes disclosing the shocked reactions of the other characters reveal that this is a grave matter, but the reader is as unaware as Martín of exactly what that problem is. The only serious incident to occur in *La colmena* is the old woman's murder; the reader's expectation is that Martín will be accused of the crime. However, there is no suggestion that this is the case. The only incontestable fact is the irony of which the reader is aware: just as Martín finally decides to join society, something dire will prevent him from accomplishing this.

La colmena selects a specific reality as a springboard, then stylizes it through the above-mentioned techniques. The distorted realism, the emphasis on the negative side of life (both connected with *tremendismo*), and the obvious author intrusion sin against the objectivity that later neorealism attempted, but the structural innovations of this work are crucial to the development of the contemporary Spanish novel: the effort to employ less direct ways of presenting the writer's opinion, the use of the multiple character and group interaction, the changing role of the reader (now forced to participate to a greater degree in the novelistic process), the emphasis on the here and now to the deliberate exclusion of psychological material or character development.

La colmena is the first of several experiments with the unanimist technique. One of Cela's more extreme examples is his *Tobogán de hambrientos* (Toboggan of hungry people, 1962),[19] which is divided into two sections: the first ("One, two, three, four, five") presents one hundred vignettes; the second ("Five, four, three, two, one") treats the same one hundred characters in reverse order. The author's extensive prologue explains his choice of form to reinforce his philosophy of contemporary behavior: "in this life everything is bound together and connected so that there is never a single loose piece" (14). This statement could easily apply to *La colmena,* as can the following excerpt, which suggests that his concern lies in the moral, rather than the social, realm: speaking of his choice of title for *Tobogán . . . ,* Cela continues, "it's the most appropriate for the slippery feeling of hunger (not physical, but rather moral hunger) of the crowd of characters who perform on their antiheroic and domestic stage" (15).

In addition to the technical innovations, Cela's use of the city as background for the fragmented portrayal of the collective protagonist is evident in other works of the period. Luis Romero's *La noria* (The waterwheel, 1952) presents fewer persons with minimal connections, except for a brief contact that facilitates the switch from one episode to another (e.g., a prostitute gets out of a cab; the story then follows the taxi driver, who arrives home and tells his daughter that it is time to get up; the third section then begins with the daughter). Further variations can be seen in Luis Goytisolo's *Las afueras* (The outskirts, 1958) or Dolores Medio's *La pez sigue flotando* (The fish stays afloat, 1959).[20]

Los bravos

Los bravos (The untamed, 1954), by Jesús Fernández Santos, is one of the works most closely associated with the Mid-Century

Generation, first because of its place as the earliest representative
novel to be written by this group,[21] second because its subject matter
and style are so illustrative of neorealism in the novel at this time.[22]
A combination of objectivist techniques with more identifiably social
concerns points the way for both ideological and stylistic interests
of other members of the neorealist group.

Los bravos is a novel of rural themes, an exposé of the stultifying,
boring, hopeless life in provincial Spain. As in *La colmena* there is
greater emphasis placed on interaction than on specifically individual dramas. Developing and waning relationships, both individual and collective, fill the novel, and, in accordance with the tenets
of objectivism, these relationships are narrated impassively, no matter how potentially dramatic the situation.[23] There are, however,
several characters whose lives stand out. Prudencio, a rich, ailing
old man, has taken a young servant-girl, Socorro, as his mistress.
The town's new doctor falls in love with her and convinces her to
leave Prudencio and live with him. The old man soon becomes
critically ill and dies. As the doctor gets to know the villagers, he
begins to ask himself what his relationship to his fellow man should
be, and whether he should remain in the town. The endless routine
is interrupted by a stranger who convinces most of the townspeople
to put their savings in an interest-bearing account. They later learn
that he is a swindler, and when he is caught only the doctor's
intervention saves him from being lynched by the outraged victims.

The town and its particular character are the real subject of *Los
bravos,* and the hopeless situation soon becomes obvious. The inhabitants hardly make an effort to raise themselves above their
present level: "What a miserable town," says don Prudencio to
himself, after seeing two little girls who he knows will inevitably
sink into the endless routine, like their mother (90–91). The doctor
thinks of the village men who, "sunk in their valley, day after day,
tried to wrench from their land a benefit which was denied to them,
struggling to return to a time of prosperity and wealth that was
not to return for them, as all things that lived do not return and,
once their destiny has been fulfilled, become decrepit" (150).

The Civil War is a minor but constant theme. Some of the
memories are gruesome (the shepherds' description of the corpses
burning [177–79]), some simply facts arising naturally in conversation. These reminders add to the negative impression of the times
in which these people have lived, with no hope for future improve-
ment and with the horror of the war still fresh enough to be relived

many times over. Descriptions of nature emphasize its merciless, capricious aspect: the oppressive heat, the annoying flies, the precariousness of the crops. These Leonese peasants are arch-victims, although the author never states this directly, and even the swindler of the novel may be another hint at their status.

The only effort toward self-improvement is one that is ultimately destructive of rural life: the abandonment of the land for the city, a practice common in the Spain of the 1950s. Emigration patterns from agricultural towns to industrial areas caused economic and social problems both in the depopulated rural areas and in the urban slums created by the population shifts.[24] This trend is documented not only in *Los bravos,* but in many novels of this period, particularly those that stressed contemporary social problems. Some examples may be seen in several of Juan Goytisolo's early novels *Fiestas* (1958) and *La resaca* (The undertow, 1958), Antonio Ferres's *La piqueta* (The pickaxe, 1959), or Ramón Nieto's *La patria y el pan* (Homeland and bread, 1962). In *Los bravos* many discussions among the townspeople center around leaving, but the problem is also situated in a wider framework. The doctor remembers stopping in an almost deserted town when he was a boy: "The people of that town had all emigrated: some to America, others, closer, within Spain. First the young people, then the old ones, called by the children who managed to make their fortune. . . . They fled from the land as if from a loathed slavery; they abandoned it and no one sowed a seed again once the cattle had been sold. . . . The doctor asked himself if it would happen again there within a few years" (111).

The novelist presents most scenes with an abundance of visual detail. Fernández Santos had studied cinematography, and the influence of this medium is evident in *Los bravos,* in verbal equivalents of the manipulation of angle, perspective, scene fade-outs, and close-ups. Instead of composing a scathing diatribe against the system responsible for such terrible conditions, Fernández Santos chooses an objectivist method to present the "facts." The narration itself is straightforward, nonjudgmental, and rather impassive. Most of the information emerges from dialogue; the connecting passages are in the third person, but the author does not take advantage of this opportunity for direct commentary.

In spite of the "objectivity" it is not difficult to uncover some symbolism in the novel. In addition to Prudencio's symbolic death, there is the paralysis of the town council president's son, whose helpless and probably incurable condition and bitter attitude epitomize the town's situation. The doctor questions whether he will stay in the region, but—despite the villagers' resentment of his protection of the swindler—he buys Prudencio's house after his death and commits himself to the town. He is obviously the only hope.[25] The "message" of the characters in *Los bravos* is complemented by another technique that allows Fernández Santos the opportunity for oblique commentary. He frequently compares the life and routine of the work animals with those of the townspeople, implying that their primitive existence is no better than that of the beasts they treat with impassivity or gratuitous cruelty.

Fernández Santos is usually parsimonious in narrative description: most characters reveal themselves only through action or dialogue, and the town, houses, and surroundings come to life mainly as functional details of daily life or as part of the characters' conversations. This deliberate avoidance of environment painting is offset by Fernández Santos's treatment of nature. While neither excessively poetic nor lyrical, the descriptions still provide a picturesque contrast with the heat and stupor of the town. One example is the doctor's long trip into the mountains to care for a sick shepherd (167 ff.).

Although Fernández Santos's novel did not have the same impact as *El Jarama*, it is one of the key works of neorealism. Rural Spain became one of the most popular settings for the social novel, which changed the focus to emphasize the backwardness and unjust treatment of the lower classes in these regions. The presentation of ordinary people with neither heroic nor even interesting qualities and the monotony of their directionless life are hallmarks of the works of this period. The use of groups rather than individuals, the "objectivity" of presentation, the lack of plot, and emphasis on dialogue are particularly associated with objectivism.[26]

El Jarama

The novel most closely associated with objectivist neorealism was published by Rafael Sánchez Ferlosio, a writer connected with the Mid-Century Generation and one of the editors of the *Revista española*. *El Jarama* (The Jarama River, published as *The One Day of the Week*) won the 1955 Nadal prize, which helped to disseminate what was for the time an unusual work and to give it publicity that increased the sales.[27]

If objectivism is to be understood as the depiction of phenomenal reality without the apparent intervention of the author, then *El Jarama* is the classic example of this interpretation of realism. Like Cela and Fernández Santos, Sánchez Ferlosio chooses the unanimist technique, presenting multiple characters within a limited spatial and temporal framework, situating them in actions and dialogues that involve only the present moment—that is, the reading time coincides closely with the novel's time.

The Jarama is a river on the outskirts of Madrid and a popular beach for the city dwellers. Particularly on Sundays, groups travel out by train to spend the day, picnic, swim, and relax. Selecting this focal point, Sánchez Ferlosio presents the activities that transpire during a single Sunday at the beach, from morning to evening. Many people form an ever-present background, but the author concentrates on two different groups, which he presents alternately: a band of young friends who work in the city and have come out for the day, and a group of older people centered in the bar-restaurant overlooking the river who are eventually joined by a taxi driver and his family later in the afternoon.

The novel simply moves from one group to another, allowing conversations to function as transmitters of necessary information and indicators of mood or tone. "Action" occurs only through the change of locale and the shifting dialogues within the scenes; these conversations are neither elegantly polished nor of transcendental or apparent symbolic interest. Rather, they provide glimpses into the everyday life and thoughts of these people, using their own preoccupations and topics of interest. The success with which *El Jarama* portrays these groups earned it the label "Epic of Banality."[28] No dramatically startling or even interesting event changes the pattern until one of the girls drowns as evening falls; a judge is called to the scene to take depositions. He and the rural police, who make sporadic appearances, are representatives of another sector: "official" Spain.

To remove himself most effectively from the novel, Sánchez Ferlosio employs dialogue to allow the characters to "present themselves," a method requiring consummate skill, given the negligible action. In the perfection of this aspect, he makes one of the most significant contributions to neorealism: a *Weltanschauung* shaped by the characters themselves. The novelist reveals an amazing versatility in imitating the various means of communication typifying each group: individual linguistic patterns and tics, country speech, city slang—all transmit commonplace topics of limited interest.[29] The astonishing accuracy of reproduction prompted some to suggest that Sánchez Ferlosio used a tape recorder or wrote the dialogues in shorthand as they were spoken, then transcribed them into book form.[30] Such criticism is a backhanded tribute to the technique of allowing the character maximum autonomy.

The neutrality of the narrative links is maintained at all times: everything may be potentially charged with significance or with no meaning at all, dependent on the perspective of the reader. One critic has even likened the narrative links between conversations to stage directions, indicting that their presence is merely functional rather than qualitative.[31] Proof of this may be seen in the nighttime drowning scene. What could have been a dramatic or pathetic event is narrated with the same impassiveness as any other situation:

> —Lucita, What are you doing out there alone? Come here to us. Luci!
>
> —She's here. Don't you see her in front of us over there? Lucita!
>
> He stopped calling in sudden fright.
>
> —Lucita!
>
> A weak struggling in the water was heard, 10, 15 meters further down, and a tight hiccough, like a strangled cry, amid panting choked in bubbles. (272)

The influence of the cinema may have suggested these techniques, which seem like the soundtrack of a documentary. Acceleration of rhythm produces a marked increase in narrative tension, a cinematographic technique used to indicate an important change of pace or emphasis.[32] Sánchez Ferlosio's firsthand acquaintance with the theoretical aspects of the neorealist cinema of Italy is seen in his translations of Lavattini for the *Revista española*.

The withdrawal of the author from overt participation in the novels imposes on the reader the task of finding the meaning—if any—that lies behind the conversations, petty squabbles, narrative links and final death. The author's role may be more limited, but it is still subtly present: the selection and arrangement of material, narrative passages that may contain a clue or symbol, connections possible between a social message that links the work to a critical perspective.[33] These possibilities, however, are left to the reader to establish, and the elevation of reader to participant effectively links character and reader in a closer relationship than is generally found in the more traditional versions of realism.

One interpretation of the meaning of *El Jarama* is based on the marked generational gap between the group of young people and the older men who are talking in the tavern. Much of the latter's conversation centers around the past, in a constant comparison between their former experiences and the present moment. The desire to live for the present and ignore or reject the past (an attitude reminiscent of the Adanic attitude of totalitarian cultural ideals)[34] is translated in the younger characters as an urge to enjoy the present fully and not worry about historical causes or future problems. The logical extension of this is a shallow, uninterested attitude toward life—possibly an oblique comment on a national situation—and a concomitant directionless philosophy of life.[35] The conversations of the younger characters are generally frivolous (concerning clothes, soccer, movies, personal relationships) and the subject of boredom arises in more than one context. Contrasting with the young people's lack of seriousness or concern with anything beyond their own limited sphere of activity, the older group reveals an understandably more mature and traditional attitude, and a concern for issues not only related to the present moment.

The theme of the Civil War is of major importance to *El Jarama*, not only in and of itself but in its function of distinguishing the two groups. Time and again the conversation returns to this subject in the obsessive memories of the older group and the refusal of the younger ones to give importance to the event. One critic interprets this lack of interest as an ideological stance against the divisive world of the previous generation,[36] while another sees their uninterest as a direct result of Falangist propaganda, which cut the younger generation from its roots by disavowing historical influences.[37]

A further group distinction may be noted in the city/country dialectic, a theme also developed by the social novelists. In *El Jarama*, the anonymity of the urban masses may be symbolized by the indistinguishability among the young city dwellers; on the other hand, the rural population has obvious personality traits, colorful nicknames, or interesting backgrounds that individualize them.[38]

Not all interpretations of this novel concentrate on the social realism of the work. A good case can be made for the symbolic value of nature in the novel: the moon has a "huge, dead face" (276), the river is "a fluid, enormous, and silent caressing animal" (271). The title alone would suggest that the river has a key role in the novel, and a close reading provides both mythical and temporal dimensions. The flow of the river may suggest the passage of human time[39] or historical time[40] (an epigraph by Da Vinci may well emphasize that theory). The river—the same, yet ever changing—may be the symbol of all of these people, who represent a wider panorama of Spanish society.

One critic sees a mythic dimension in the personification of the Jarama, who, like a cruel god, demands the sacrifice of a city person every year.[41] Another finds transcendental symbols: the spiral image in such forms as a bicycle wheel suggests the wheel of fortune; the fish Luci swallowed when in the water earlier foretells her tragic death; dancing symbolizes the dance of death.[42]

El Jarama has been hailed as one of the landmarks of the postwar novel because it undertook new stylistic and thematic directions. Darío Villanueva points out its innovations: the banal themes, the reproduction of colloquial language, the lack of plot, and the identification of the characters within a social group.[43] Many of these traits appear in such diverse works as *Gran sol* (Great Sole, 1957, by Ignacio Aldecoa), *La Zanja* (The trench, 1961, by Alfonso Grosso), *Tormenta de verano* (*Summer Storm*, 1961, by García Hortelano), and *La piqueta* (The pickaxe, 1959, by Antonio Ferres).

Chapter Six
The Social Novel

The social novel is the most controversial of the three modes of Spanish neorealism. Particularly in vogue during the 1950s and 1960s, it concentrates on phenomena closely associated with the times in which it is written. This preference in turn defines three major characteristics: the use of the chronological present (both in the story and in reference to the actual time period in which the novel is set); regional or urban Spain as locale; and socioeconomic problems as preferred themes. These problems are generally presented full-blown, with no effort to trace causes. The historical perspective is deliberately omitted.[1]

This problem-orientation separates the social novelists from the other two branches of neorealism. For the social writer, content and message take priority over other considerations. One of these authors states, "The novel should be connected to national reality . . . it should fulfill an obvious social function, independent of its purely literary values."[2] This is not to say that the other branches of neorealism ignored social implications. On the contrary, they manifest their "commitment" time and again, but their interpretation of "social" (which may range from vaguely humanitarian sentiments to accusatory political opinions) is not as restrictive as that of the social writers. Each group had its particular way of dealing with contemporary problems: the objectivists took a sociological tack, while relying less on obviously critical situations; the subjective realists universalize the implications of their "criticism," although the examples may apply to their own period. In the case of the social novel, the primary intention is to present a critical view of contemporary Spanish social, economic, and political reality. Employed as a tool to denounce unfair conditions, injustice, lack of progress, and so on, the social novel became a type of exposé—not the chronicle of transformation as in the case of the earlier traditional novel, but an "impassive" compilation of the wrongs perpetrated on certain segments of society. There is ample evidence that this group intended to present such conditions under critical light with the hope that some change could be effected as a result.[3]

Precedents are found in the later novels of Blasco Ibáñez and in the prewar social novel, such as the works of Ramón J. Sender (b. 1902)—*O.P. (Orden público)* (Law and order, 1931) or *Siete domingos rojos (Seven Red Sundays,* 1932). Sender was joined by others interested in the direction and possibilities of social literature, which was dubbed "New Romanticism" by the critical spokesman of that generation.[4] Of particular interest to these earlier writers was the conflict of the lower classes with either the official political machine or with the upper class. The orientation of these novels is evident in representative titles not only by Sender, but by other writers: César M. Arconada's *La Turbina* (The turbine, 1930) and *Los pobres contra los ricos* (The poor against the rich, 1933) or Joaquín Arderíus's *Campesinos* (Peasants, 1931). One of the greatest differences between the prewar and postwar works, however, is the deliberate intrusion of the author in the earlier works, in rhetorical sections (apotheoses, direct address, etc.) or lyrical passages.

Allusions to ideological or theoretical programs during the 1940s and 1950s point to a committed attitude, but there is some difficulty in pinpointing exact sources. Goytisolo mentions Marxist ideology as one of the influences on the generation;[5] other critics cite Sartre, Lukacs, Brecht, Goldmann, Barthes, Marx, and Engels as possible or definite influences.[6] There is no doubt that Lukacs's theories were familiar to Spanish writers by 1959, when Vittorini used his ideas as the basis for a presentation at the Formentor Colloquium. Both Lukacs and Brecht were cited at a conference in 1962.[7] Documents from the period seem to suggest that political issues followed rather than directed the artistic bases of the works.[8]

Social realism had several creditable and outspoken defenders in its early years. José María Castellet and Juan Goytisolo analyzed and encouraged its ideology and technique (see above, pp. 30–31) explaining its characteristics, praising its fidelity to reality and its apparent lack of identification with bourgeois conventions. Castellet both promoted the new writers and defended the social consciousness of the authors. Other critics, especially Ricardo Doménech, offered favorable analyses of the writers in columns published in respectable journals and newspapers.

Several factors gave cohesiveness to the social novelists. They published in *Acento cultural,* a journal that defended realism and the connection between literature and society. Two publishing houses helped to launch the novelists by publicizing the movement with literary prizes: Destino with the Nadal prize, Seix Barral with the Biblioteca Breve prize. Carlos Barral (a key figure in the promotion of several literary movements) also arranged for their foreign distribution. The European readers received these novels with interest, and Spanish social literature was quite popular for a time.[9]

Since the major concern of the social novel is situational exposé, one approach to the analysis of the movement is through its thematic constants. Three general themes appear time and again, singly or in combination: regional experiences (rural and urban), problems arising from work, and class or group conflicts.

In typical works of regional or rural orientation, the protagonists are from the lower classes—specifically, the peasant farmers or lower-class workers, identified with regional-related jobs. These novels reveal the misery, poverty, and often hopeless conditions of the area: lack of education, modern-day conveniences, modern farming equipment. Their plight is exacerbated by being at the mercy of both nature (unpredictable weather affecting crops; severe weather causing intolerable living conditions) and exploitation by employers who take advantage of their lack of mobility. José Manuel Caballero Bonald's *Dos días de setiembre* (Two days in September, 1962) portrays viniculture in the Andalusian region; *La zanja* (The ditch, 1961, by Alfonso Grosso) describes a social cross-section of the population of a small Andalusian town during a single day; *La huelga* (The strike, 1967) by Luisa Isabel Alvarez de Toledo, Duchess of Medina Sidonia, confronts upper and lower class in southern Spain. Unjust and uncaring *caciques* (political or regional bosses) or rich landowners often appear in exploitive roles, as in *El cacique* (The boss, 1963), by Luis Romero and *La noche más caliente* (The hottest night, 1965), by Daniel Sueiro.

A variation on this theme is the unexpected appearance of an outside force, such as a big business or a technical project ostensibly sent in to improve the lives of the rural population. Invariably the very people whom this is to help end up as the victims (intentionally or not), indicating that such provisional changes are not satisfactory; rather they must emerge slowly and thoughtfully from an entire reworking of the socioeconomic system. A case in point is *Central eléctrico* (Powerhouse, 1958), Jesús López Pacheco's description of the installation of a powerhouse to bring light (meant in a symbolic as well as a material sense) to the region. The reader learns of the backward conditions of the town (which is eventually flooded), the displacement of its inhabitants, and their subsequent victimization because of the nature of their relocation.

Particularly characteristic of the rural setting are touches of local color that complement the theme. The effort to reproduce a scene, almost in tableau fashion, is reminiscent of such rural *costumbristas* as Estébanez Calderón: in this mode, the reader accompanies the author as an outsider whose attention is focused on details one by one as if viewing them for the first time. In the social novel, the ironic, humorous tone of the earlier writers becomes an impassive listing of the miserable or backward conditions or, at the very least, details that bolster the illusion of documentation. The extensive use of regional dialect is another way of making the reader aware of the class and area associated with the speaker. These sketches are a type of social *costumbrismo,* as much aware of itself as the model, but with an entirely different purpose. [10]

Inefficient land management, poor economic conditions, and the lack of opportunity to better oneself are causes of dislocation, with its subsequent tragic consequences. Those novels treating emigration within Spanish borders also describe causative factors in Andalusia or other agricultural areas: primitive farming conditions, poor land, lack of work, and the unjust landowner system force the lower class to relocate. *La mina* (The mine, 1960), by Armando López Salinas, for example, follows one family from an agricultural to a mining community; much of its pathos derives from the constant measuring of events against their beloved home. Angel María de Lera's *Tierra para morir* (Land to die on, 1964) also treats the emigration problem and the consequent desertion of rural towns. Pathos generally accompanies the theme of separation—not only from one's family and friends but from one's very roots and culture. Such is the case in Ramón Solís's *Ajena crece la hierba* (Alien grows the grass, 1962), the story of a Spanish worker in France. Several novels concentrate on those Spaniards who emigrate to Germany: *El sol no sale para todos* (The sun doesn't rise for everyone, 1966), Juan José Rodero's chronicle of an office employee; or Angel María de Lera's *Hemos perdido el sol* (We have lost the sun, 1963).

Emigration patterns also provide the opportunity to introduce the second "regional" concern of the social novelist: life in the city. Those novels that concentrate on urban experience often elaborate on the miserable life of the emigrant from the country, on the sense of displacement as the anonymity of city life engulfs the uprooted people, who live in the slums in shacks (*chabolas*) under the most primitive conditions. "Chabolismo" offers a magnificent theme for those who wish to present incontrovertible evidence of the separation between the haves and the have-nots. Madrid is the target of many of these works: Antonio Ferres's *La Piqueta* (The pickaxe, 1959); Angel María de Lera's *Los olvidados* (The forgotten ones, 1957); Ramón Nieto's *La patria y el pan* (Homeland and bread, 1962). Juan Goytisolo paints Barcelona's slums in *La resaca* (The undertow, 1958) and other works. The horrifying conditions of this sector appear as secondary themes in García Hortelano's *Nuevas amistades* (New friendships, 1959) or Martín-Santos's *Tiempo de silencio* (*Time of Silence,* 1962), in which the upper class makes a brief foray into another "world."

The housing shortage is another major concern to the social novelists, who describe the unhappy search for adequate shelter, evictions, the necessity for subletting. Housing problems generally appear in urban novels, whether as an ancillary to other concerns, as in *Funcionario público* (Public servant, 1956), by Dolores Medio, or *Esta oscura desbandada* (This dark disbandment, 1952), by Zunzunegui, or as primary theme, as in *En plazo* (On time, 1961), by Fernando Avalos, or *El desahucio* (Eviction, 1963), by Severiano Fernández Nicolás.[11]

The city may also serve as a symbol of the depressing years of postwar Spain, with all the misery, selfishness and victimization associated with this period. In *Esta oscura desbandada*, Zunzunegui employs traditional novelistic techniques, but the climate of desperation and exploitation and the criticism of the middle class certainly situate him on the fringe of a social concern. More to the point is Armando López Salinas's *Año tras año* (Year after year, 1962), an exposé of the terrible postwar years symbolized by life in the city (Madrid) and oppression of the working class; Francisco Umbral's *Travesía de Madrid* (Across Madrid, 1966) also presents city life in an unflattering light.

Less wedded to a specific region, the job-oriented novel portrays the worker's problems: low wages, dangerous working conditions, difficulties of rising in employment or moving to better jobs. The office worker or minor public servant, a subject of Spanish social realism from Galdós's *Miau* (1888) through Enrique Azcoaga's *El empleado* (The employee, 1949), reappears in such novels as Dolores Medio's *Funcionario público* and Daniel Sueiro's *La criba* (The sieve, 1961), both of which treat human problems aggravated by poor wages and depressing conditions. *La mina* describes work in the Spanish mines by focusing upon the life of an emigrated campesino; *Tren minero* (Mining train, 1965), by José Antonio Parra, develops the same theme. The less glamorous aspects of bullfighting are exposed in Angel María de Lera's *Los clarines del miedo* (*The Horns of Fear*, 1958), and some social interest is seen in *Gran sol* (Great Sole, 1957), Ignacio Aldecoa's epic of deep-sea fishermen.

Since most plots elaborate on the economic problems of the lower classes, there is considerable emphasis accorded to money. Food—or its lack—receives parallel treatment. The concern with what they eat (or do not eat), the exaggerated attention to a single, tempting (and often unattainable) item, and the exact description of the plain, functional fare of the poor compared to the more substantial or even sumptuous meals of the more fortunate are the most prevalent ways in which this motif appears. For example, a telling contrast between rich and poor appears in *La mina:* "They don't work and they have good bread, oil, wine and meat; for the rest, crumbs and *gazpacho.*"[12]

The third typical area of exploration in the social novel is collective behavior. Inequality becomes particularly obvious when seen through detailed presentations of a group's characteristics and the contrasts between classes. The tendency of social neorealism to associate the individual with his group is in part a result of the documentary intentions of the movement. A sense of collective experience infuses the action, and the protagonist thus becomes the illustration of the plight of an entire group. The experience of the main character is reinforced by similar or parallel episodes involving others in the same predicament (for example, the various workers' stories of *La mina,* or the deplorable circumstances of the many people of the lower class in *La zanja).* The emphasis on the representative features of the main character often requires reduction of his unique personal qualities. Man is seen in contact with historical forces, not in a particular human dimension.

The relationship of the reader to the text is that of onlooker, with no more privileged information than what he gleans from the actions or words that he "witnesses." Protagonists may present themselves "directly," either through conversations or interior monologues. Combined with the reduction of character uniqueness, such "objectivity" prevents the reader's identification with a single person but gives him a keener sense of the problem at hand and the role the character plays in it. In the most successful cases, the novelist does not sacrifice personality to an ideological abstraction and there is a skillful merging of individual psychology and collective problems (such as in *Dos días de setiembre*). Less creative writers produce flat, one-dimensional, or uninteresting protagonists in the social novel.[13]

Individual motivations are generally absent in those novels that concentrate on class or group characteristics. Contact between the lower and middle/upper classes or between labor and management offers a potentially emotional or inflammatory situation. In either case, the weaker component of the pair is emotionally, physically, or economically exploited, with the clear implication that he is the eternal victim. This may be the case in the company, or "boss," versus the employee (*La mina, La Zanja, El Suceso* [The event, 1965, by José Antonio Vizcaíno]), or the contact between upper and lower classes (*Oficio de muchachos* [Boys' job, 1963, by Manuel Arce], or Ramón Nieto's *El sol amargo* [Bitter sun, 1961], which deals with tourism), or between landowners or *señoritos* and the peasant class (*La fiebre, La mina,* etc.).

If the collective plight of these victims is intended to evoke indignation and pity, even to the point of bathos, the irresponsibility of the upper classes, stylized to the point of caricature, with even fewer motivations for behavior (except for greed and hypocrisy) than their victims, is supposed to provoke loathing. One of the greatest defects of the social novel is that it exaggerates the dialectic of proletariat-capitalist, victim-exploiter, worker-manager, or individual-bureaucracy, and reduces individual characteristics to conform to ideological schemata, which has been attacked by critics of the social novel, who find the naive, Manichaean divisions unsatisfactory.[14]

One group of interest to the social writers (although they preferred to avoid politically sensitive situations) is the losers of the Civil War. Both conception and style determine whether this subject falls within the bounds of social realism: some writers individualize the problem and use it in a symbolic sense, thus completely removing it from the intent of the social novel. Antonio Ferres's *Los vencidos* (The losers, 1965) details executions, reprisals, and the plight of the political prisoner in the postwar era. For obvious reasons, it was published in France; another work printed outside Spain, Daniel Sueiro's *Estos son tus hermanos* (These are your brothers, 1965), describes the return of a political exile and the hostile reception he receives in his hometown.

The middle and upper classes are also the targets of class-related exposés. Juan Goytisolo seems particularly fascinated with the subject of class and generational conflicts. Repeatedly in his early novels, a sensitive individual undergoes a series of adventures that determine his fate while simultaneously defining contemporary social problems. His first work, *Juegos de manos* (Sleight of hand, published as *The Young Assassins*, 1954), depicts a group of bourgeois youth who decide that a gratuitous act of murder would give definition to their rebellion against their parents and the older generation. In his desire to belong, a more sensitive youth becomes tragically enmeshed in the scheme. More purposeless in their lives are the protagonists of Juan Marsé's *Encerrados con un solo juguete* (Shut up with a single toy, 1960); here political undertones parallel a life of frustrated adolescent rebellion in two families. Marsé's *Esta cara de la luna* (This face of the moon, 1962) also describes a youth who fails in his idealistic rebellion. Juan Antonio Payno's *El curso* (The course, 1962) offers another example of the lack of direction, this time in university students.

The older generation receives even more scathing treatment, sometimes to the point of caricature, in such works as *Requiem para todos nosotros* (Requiem for us all, 1968), José María Sanjuan's interpretation of the life of the jetsetters; Angel María de Lera's *Trampa* (Trap, 1962); or Manuel Arce's *El precio de la derrota* (The price of losing, 1970). Constant drinking, love affairs, a continual round of parties, and petty jealousies characterize their empty lives. The details of some of these novels were so graphic that critics questioned their veracity and purpose, with the clear suggestion that this was a high-class "Novela rosa" written with less than honorable intentions. [15]

The social novelists favor a direct, expositional technique on the part of the author-witness, who presents a descriptive picture of what he observes (it is called by one critic *novela de presentación*), the exception being the character's self-presentation through thoughts or interior monologue. The procedures used to convey the conditions in Spain are very simple. The plot is uncomplicated and lineal. There is minimal interference of literary devices to distract the reader from the problem or to make him aware of the artistic framework that is supporting it. The main narrative tools in the social novel are dialogue (a "natural" way to inform the reader of the circumstances) and description. The latter is straightforward, expository, and may become painstakingly detailed in descriptions of work processes or living conditions, thus providing an impression of documentation. Great care is taken to present the conditions fully, because judgments are not proffered by the author, but are to arise from the situation. In most cases, the point of view is that of the observer, which the reader shares.

In keeping with the effort to maintain documentary realism, the social neorealists create the impression of verisimilitude by reproducing conversation appropriate to the level of the speaker. Since many of the characters in these novels are lower-class people identified with a specific region, writers take great pains to convey peculiar linguistic patterns. Slang, dialect, regionalisms, mispronunciations, poor grammar—even inarticulateness—form part of the popular lexicon of these characters. Certain social novelists abuse this linguistic element, however,[16] as critics of the movement have pointed out. The effort to dissociate themselves from prose that was too ornate, conceptual, or "literary" is overdone in some cases, to the point of being counterproductive of the effect desired.

Social neorealism declined after a period of intense exploration of its possibilities. In this case, however, the reaction against it was considerably more virulent than usual, since the very authors who touted its theories now repudiated them. One reason for the rapid waning in popularity was disapproval on the part of European literati, who gave unexpectedly harsh reviews of García Hortelano's prize-winning *Tormenta de verano*.[17] This "rejection" by former European fans coincided with the introduction of Spanish American magic realism and experimental literature, introduced by the very publishing company that had promoted social literature. Further, intellectuals turned toward new experimental literature within Spain, such as the 1962 *Tiempo de silencio (Time of Silence),* which coupled the best of social concerns with an intellectual, subjective approach to literature.

As these new literary currents began to gain popularity, and other influences changed the focus of the novel, many authors moved from a social stance to more experimental writing (Caballero Bonald, Goytisolo, Ferres). Some critics finally repudiated the social novel entirely, dismissing it as more document than literature, with a very limited scope, characterizing it with such derogatory epithets as "school of the beet," to emphasize its humble thematics,[18] and even the staunchest defenders of the social novel saw it now with more experienced eyes, complaining of its uninspired language, the use of literature for a political tool, the monotony of approach.[19] Descriptions such as "simplistic and mechanical acceptance of reality," "gray," and "sterile," were applied, and some insinuated that the position of the author was also false—that is, his middle-class origin hindered him from experiencing the subjects he was writing about, resulting in an intellectual position lacking authenticity.[20]

Social literature never ceased publication, although the vanguard moved on to new territory. In his excellent two-volume study on the social novel, Sanz Villanueva provides titles of collections and individual works that show a continued interest in its possibilities, although its tenets no longer seem compelling and it lacks the cohesiveness of early years.

La mina

Armando López Salinas's *La mina* (The mine, 1960), one of the better prototypes of social realism published in this period,[21] studies a number of social and economic problems on an individual and national level, approaching the question mainly through a documentary perspective. *La mina* describes the hardships with which the Andalusian peasant farmer exists, a situation illustrated by Joaquín, whose efforts to make a living are systematically frustrated. In desperation, he leaves the land he loves to take employment in a mine, where he works under terrible conditions and finally is killed in a cave-in. *La mina* explores three themes of particular concern to the social novelist: the intolerable economic conditions in southern Spain, internal emigration patterns and their consequences, and the exploitation of workers. The constant ancillary to these problems is the inflexible and avaricious position of the capitalist owners and their representatives.

Although Joaquín is the main protagonist, López Salinas assures the representational significance of the individual drama by multiplying examples. The longest section ("The Crew") introduces mining procedures and life in the mining village. The reader learns that the shafts are poorly ventilated and thick with dust, the wooden supports are rotten, the heat is intense, hardly any light is provided for digging, and human filth and debris are everywhere. Finally, the description of a miner's life suggests a hopeless cycle: emigration to the mine, dreadful conditions, the desire of the new arrival to leave as soon as he has earned enough money, subsequent bad health, and apathy, all of which finally prevent him from leaving (96). In direct contrast, the portrayal of the middle and upper class reveals an unsympathetic attitude toward the workers' plight, a selfishness that seems to be a universal trait. Blatant exploitation is associated with the practices of the mining company, which forces a sick man to go back to work, encourages spying on fellow workers' activities, and not only refuses to heed the legitimate warnings of the miners concerning the unsafe conditions but even punishes them for complaining. The cave-in that kills Joaquín's crew is a direct result of the firm's evasion of responsibility.

Balancing the condemnation of the selfish attitude of those upon whom the workers must depend is an equally sympathetic concern for the predicament of the lower class. In addition to the "objective" examples of Joaquín's miserable situation, López Salinas introduces elements of pathos that make the final tragedy even more dreadful. The horses used in the mine are clear parallels of the men, who are treated like beasts. Descriptions insist on the connection between animals and men: "There is even someone worse off than the miners. The mine horses never leave the tunnels. . . . After two or three years their lungs are full of stones, they breathe like old women and work two shifts. . . . On hearing the last sound of the siren [the horses] got up as if they were workmen" (89). As Joaquín works with them for the first time, he reinforces the parallel: "Surely we will be good friends" (89). The horses perish with the men at the end of the novel. Immediately before the cave-in, Joaquín tells the horses in great detail about his plans for buying and working the land. His elaborate plans alternate with descriptions of the dirt and asphyxiating atmosphere in the mine (223 ff.).

The manner in which López Salinas depicts Joaquín (the representative of his class) and the overseers (who symbolize the middle and upper classes) establishes a clear opposition: the noble, downtrodden worker versus the capitalists who exploit him. This opposition may well be true of contemporary life, but its literary depiction goes to extremes to make its point.

As Gil Casado notes, one edition of *La mina* describes a rebellion against the company following the cave-in.[22] In the censored version, however, the ending is rather more hopeful. After a period of intense mourning, Joaquín's wife realizes that life must continue, even though her fate is exile from the land they loved (247). Thus she makes the decision to remain in the mining village, breaking the cycle of emigration. "Seeing the little ones, she felt a great peace and a calm serenity. A serenity that arose from deep within, from her hope" (247). These are the final words of *La mina*. The pathetic elements still remain (the woman's suffering, her exile, the courage with which she confronts her future), but the resignation with which she accepts the tragedy seems inappropriate in light of the chronicle of injustices suffered by the family.[23] The closing pages deal exclusively with the wife; López Salinas's concentration on one person alone—not the usual accumulation of examples—may symbolize her utter solitude. But if the reader is to assume that she represents the survivors of the tragedy, then the author seems to indicate that nothing can be done to change the nature of the situation. If the author meant to present a simple exposé (a documentary, rather than a call to action), he has accomplished his task well. The remarks by Gil Casado concerning the censored version may well bear out the fact that the author had no choice in the way the novel was to end.

Dos días de setiembre

José Manuel Caballero Bonald's *Dos días de setiembre* (Two days in September, Biblioteca Breve prize, 1961)[24] provides an excellent example of a social novel whose literary qualities complement its functional purpose. It falls into the category of job-related works and portrays the operations, responsibilities, and problems of those connected with viniculture. However, the professional aspect is simply one part of a complex interrelationship of class, character, type, sex, business, and historical period. Each of the categories has its main exponent, whose representational quality is reinforced through secondary characters emphasizing the collective aspect through repetitive or mirroring devices and incidents. In addition, the person assumes an individuality that transcends the group he represents.

The limited temporal frame suggested by the title parallels an equally restrictive spatial frame—a small Andalusian town[25] during vintage season, a time that shapes part of the internal movement.

The novel opens with the frustrated nocturnal attempt of Lucas and Joaquín to steal some grapes, a desperate action conveying the extent of their poverty and the fact that the riches of the land belong to very few. Joaquín (a man without a country, in many senses) tries desperately to find work, either during the vintage or occasionally as a *cantaor* (flamenco singer). His poverty, unhappiness, and inability to obtain employment are perhaps caused by his association with the losing side of the Civil War, a fact that has been neither forgotten nor forgiven. Although he has served his time in jail, an intransigent mayor refuses to give him his papers and ejects him from his hometown. His existence becomes that of an outsider, and his accidental death (he is crushed by a wine barrel) constitutes the ironic finale in the life of an archetypal victim. Even in death he is persecuted: the police refuse to shelter his body from the rain and beat Lucas for begging them to move it.

If Joaquín's role in life is to be a loser, the fate of the middle-class *señorito* may be more comfortable but is of no better quality. Miguel, who realizes that his life is purposeless, spends his evenings drinking and carousing, and his days half-drunk or nursing a hangover. "The sheets I cover myself with weigh me down, the ballast of still undigested old wine. . . . I've got to do something, I've got to grab on to a burning nail and do something to get out of this god-awful hole that keeps dragging me down into my stupid and miserable betrayal" (118). Friends with whom he associates are equally directionless and are characterized by their constant drinking, superficial attitudes, and interest in sensual satisfaction. Rafael is a particularly good foil, with his self-disgust because of his propensity for women.

The power base of the town is found in the rich landowners, each of whom suffers from some type of defect. The effeminate don Andrés feels guilty at having so much money and arranges to pay for a dinner for the poor people of the town. Felipe, a "respectable" town citizen, takes advantage of helpless people: he has raped a girl and, as Miguel's guardian, squandered much of his inheritance. Don Gabriel takes advantage of the female servants in his house, and when he sees a young girl who interests him he is not above arranging to have her "work" for him.

For a work with such a realistic base, the absence of extensive physical description is noteworthy. Caballero Bonald prefers to use a single trait as novelistic shorthand, which both identifies and symbolizes the character. Don Andrés is effeminate; the greedy shopkeeper, Ayuso, is dirty and his wife is slovenly; Lola (Joaquín's companion) is careless about her appearance. Joaquín is identified constantly with a large wen on his temple, the mark of Cain or of a scapegoat. In contrast, there is considerably greater emphasis on the surroundings, an important indicator of the life of the characters. Joaquín's pitiful room, dominated by a huge bed; Ayuso's filthy store; the luxurious surroundings to which don Gabriel wakes up in the morning—are all details that confirm the life-style of each individual and emphasize the class separation.

While there is not a great deal of linear movement in the plot, frequent interaction among the people gives the impression of constant activity. Such contacts may occur only between two people or take place in the several scenes in the tavern, at the vineyard, or in the tenement, all testifying to the type of life in the town. There are even some *costumbrista* touches, as in the conversation around the water spigot in the tenement house. This realism is enhanced by speech filled with slang, job-, or sports-related vocabulary. Several sections deal with the technicalities of wine-making, but they are artistically integrated into the novel, as in Miguel's interior monologue, which alternates between a textbook description of vini-culture and the remembrance of his past (209–20). There is also a detailed account of the dangerous job of stacking the huge wine barrels, which also serves as a preparation for the final accident. The regional focus and choice of seasonal time frame justify the use of this technical vocabulary as a natural part of the novel.

The separate strands of personal and work-related situations are woven together to culminate in Joaquín's death, which also coincides with the breaking out of a storm and with the admission of two of the protagonists of their failures: Miguel's guilt at not having lived up to his potential and Ayuso's shame at his avarice.

Caballero Bonald has expressed his interest in the social function of the novel: "Spain's reality is within the reach of everyone who wishes to look at it and understand it. I have reflected that reality with the greatest objectivity possible. It is sufficient to do that for the novel to fulfill a social function of authentic political capacity, testifying to each and every one of the circumstances of man situated in Spanish history."[26]

Caballero Bonald clearly felt the influence of the objectivist novel, whose theories were well known at the time he wrote *Dos días*, but the particular selection of the various social levels, the caricature of the rich upper classes (effeminacy, lechery, greed), and the obvious attempt at representational character functions reveal more of the author's hand than he thinks. Nonetheless, his combination of aesthetic and social concerns, a careful balancing of techniques and styles, his use of leitmotifs (the weather, the wine), and his attempt to insure some psychological individuality make this novel an outstanding example of social neorealism as well as a work of universal human and literary concerns.

Travel Literature

An unusual "subgenre" related to the social novel emerged with the travel books published during the period of the social novel. The mode was introduced by Cela in 1948 with his *Viaje a la Alcarria* (*Journey to the Alcarria*), the product of his "discovery" of rural Spain. Following his example, young writers began taking walking tours through various regions of their country, chronicling Spanish reality for their readers. "Travel literature" may suggest glossy tourist guides recommending picturesque qualities of the area, but nothing could be further from these works. Most, in fact, conform to the intention of the social novel in their criticism of the backward conditions of the regions they describe. Many are literary exposés of a way of life that had received little attention and are a hybrid genre, utilizing characteristics of both essay and fiction.[27]

Although ideologically the Generation of 1898 offers the closest connection with this pseudotravel literature, the technique of the *costumbrista* writers is evident in descriptions that are often picturesque and related with great detail, emphasizing the fact that the writer considered the region to be "foreign" to the Spanish way of life. The faithful transcription of dialogue and the emphasis on local customs and sayings are typical of the social novel, which added unpleasant truths about Spanish reality to the quaint details of *costumbrismo*.

Camilo José Cela's *Viaje a la Alcarria*[28] is the earliest example of contemporary travel literature. It is a chronicle of a trip taken on foot in 1946 interspersed with selective descriptions of the area and the people in it. The narration about a third-person "traveler" creates an aesthetic distance that places the "traveler" on the same level with the people he encounters and allows Cela the author to include

Cela the traveler as well as his other subjects in an ironic overlay. The traveler leaves Madrid early one morning to take the train to his destination. The darkness enveloping him and the unsavory or unhappy characters he sees en route to the train portray the city in an evil and menacing light. Each chapter offers new places and experiences, which he narrates in quick visual sketches laced with realistic details: people, animals, the countryside. Much of the book is devoted to conversations between the traveler and the people he meets, affording Cela ample opportunity to display his virtuosity in conveying picturesque and earthy speech peppered with popular sayings.

Viaje a la Alcarria is not a social work of denunciation with a program for change. Rather, it is a chronicle of rural Spain, a revelation of human nature in all of its misery and glory—the contemporary interpretation of Unamuno's *intrahistoria*. Cela's usual cast of characters is present: beggars, children, the retarded, and so on, their innocence and defenselessness contrasting plainly with the more mundane, egoistic tendencies of their fellow men. Cela's fondness for the picturesque—through anecdotes, nicknames, earthy expressions—brings the region and its people to life. His interest in the past—as a psychological as well as a historical factor— removes him from the mainstream of social literature. *Viaje a la Alcarria* raises travel literature to a high artistic level and, despite Cela's protestations that it is a "geography book,"[29] stands as more proof of his literary talent and a tribute to his originality. He has continued to produce travel books, changing the place, modifying the focus, but none compares in quality and freshness of outlook to his first work.

Later writers, particularly those of the Mid-Century Generation, adapted the tradition of travel literature to their own ends. Singly or in pairs, they covered almost every region in Spain, and as they wrote they altered the literary emphasis of Cela, making the trip a documentary, whose more exact description of external reality is reinforced, in many cases, by "conversations" with the people, with photographs as supporting evidence. Thus the emphasis shifts from essentially human characteristics to a critique of contemporary rural Spain: misery, poverty, hunger, lack of education, unsanitary conditions, and, of course, the unproductive, hostile land and the passive resignation of its inhabitants. The emphasis on the external ambience as a means of criticism prompted one critic to ask whether some of these works deserved to be included in a literary study, proof that their intention had changed radically from that of Cela's original work.[30] The shift in emphasis is visible in the preface to some of the works. Cela begins, "The traveler leaves full of good intentions: he intends to scratch the surface of the heart of the man on the road, to look at the soul of the travelers . . ." (21). Twelve years later, Antonio Ferres and Armando López Salinas commenced another travel book in this manner: "The knowledge of how the people of our country live, think, and work should lead us to a greater and better social understanding of the problems of our time, in Spain as it is today"[31]—the intention of *Caminando por las Hurdes* (Walking through Hurdes, 1960). Other travel books of note—not by any means an all-inclusive list[32]—are Juan Goytisolo's *Campos de Níjar* (Fields of Nijar, 1960) and *La Chanca* (1962), grim pictures of the region around Almería, and Antonio Ferres's *Tierra de olivos* (Land of the olive trees, 1964).

Chapter Seven
Subjective Neorealism

Even the briefest overview of contemporary Spanish literature confirms the realist mode as the single constant factor, but it also reveals the elasticity with which the writers interpret reality throughout these years. Both objectivism and the social novel strive to depict life "exactly" as it is, using a documentary or empirical approach to the subject. They carefully record surface phenomena with a minimal personal dimension.

A less objective interpretation of reality also appears during the period of neorealism. It is variously called critical realism, intimate realism, poetic realism, psychological realism, or personal realism, all terms that acknowledge the presence of a transcendent dimension in these works. I prefer the term "subjective realism" because it suggests the evident hand of the writer in the work. Subjective neorealism still selects an identifiable reality for its point of departure, but both technique and perspective differ substantially from objectivist and social concerns. The subjective writers develop a synchronic vision as they filter the action through an individual viewpoint, deliberately penetrating surface appearance to reveal a multidimensional reality. To accomplish this, they replace the "impersonal" reportage of the other modes of neorealism with a rich variety of literary and structural elements.

Much of subjective neorealism shares the critical stance of the social novel, particularly its disapproval of middle-class values and behavior, but adds to it a human dimension that expands these concerns beyond the specific socioeconomic or historical factor. Instead, it examines constants of human behavior and condemns bad faith, hypocrisy, cruelty, and egoism. One of the writer-critics has defended and defined this expanded sense of reality typical of his group in this way: "The mission of realism taken as an aesthetic current is that of taking literature from life, and not life from life—the case with *costumbrismo,* with the documentary novel."[1] The social neorealists are grouped around a common view of the function of literature; the objectivist writers are loosely connected by stylistic concerns. The subjective neorealists, however, do not lend themselves so easily either to thematic or stylistic categorization, but, for the purpose of understanding the variations on neorealism during the postwar period, several generalizations are offered below that signal common interests and literary practices of the subjective neorealists.

The most striking difference between subjective neorealism and the more objective modes is the return of the individual to a place of preeminence: his personal problems, relationships, emotions, and development override the social issues and the representative characters identified with the latter. The protagonist may serve as spokesman or alter ego for the author, or as symbol of a situation about which the author may wish to comment. A concomitant expansion of the interior dimension accompanies this narrowed focus, and often the reader finds a major portion of the plot devoted to the elaboration of a psychological attitude or awareness, or to a conflict between the inner world and objective reality. The basic sense of dialectic is still maintained, but the emphasis shifts from opposing social forces to the dissonance between interior life, ideals, and hope and the various manifestations of social or historical existence. This is the point at which the social novel and subjective neorealism may intersect.

Most of these characters are estranged from the society in which they live, whose values and behavioral patterns they cannot or do not wish to share. Thus strange, abnormal, or alienated people take the role of main protagonists, expressing their separation from conventional existence, which the author shows as unsatisfactory. The child character is particularly appropriate—and prevalent—in these cases, since the author can manipulate a naive or innocent viewpoint discovering with astonishment how unpleasant reality can be. Initiation into adult society is often the result of a traumatic experience, in which the false security of the childhood world is shattered, leaving the character in the disillusioned, solitary, and alienated state so typical of this movement. Young adolescents also convey this symbolic division: confrontation with adults erodes or shatters their ideals. Some try to rebel by a decisive, often gratuitous act, by death or withdrawal from a world they refuse to accept.

The list of young protagonists in this group is particularly lengthy (perhaps a reflection of the authors' obsession with their own childhood). Miguel Delibes's *El camino* (*The Path,* 1950) is a bittersweet novel of a young boy who reminisces about his childhood the night before he is to leave for schooling in the city. The humor and freshness of life in a small town as interpreted by a child make pleasant reading, but beyond the apparently carefree boyhood adventures lie progress, the city, and adulthood. *El camino* is laced with natural symbols, associating nature with a type of prelapsarian wonder and innocence, yet the boy's departure and the death of a boyhood friend suggest the passing of an entire way of life. Still rural, but decidedly less idyllic, is Delibes's *Las ratas* (The rats, published as *Smoke on the Ground*, 1962), which describes an unusual child and the sordid environment that surrounds him—an excellent example of the balance of social concerns (the primitive conditions of the Castilian town) with the development of the individual personality. Juan Goytisolo's *Duelo en el Paraíso* (Mourning in Paradise, published as *Children of Chaos*, 1955) presents a group of refugee children who create their own version of the ongoing Civil War by playing war games and executing one of the younger members, an "outsider" named Abel. The title and the boy's name associate the historical reality with a universal paradigm. Many of Goytisolo's early works follow the maturation of a particularly sensitive adolescent against the background of peer pressure (*Juegos de manos*, 1954) or unpleasant social reality (*Fiestas*, 1958). Luis Castresana's *El otro árbol de Guernica* (Guernica's other tree, 1967) places children within the context of the Civil War, a popular theme with these writers. Most of Ana María Matute's works unfold the unpleasant rite of passage from childhood to adolescence or from adolescence to adulthood. Some characters experience the inevitable disappearance of their ideals (*Primera memoria* [Early memories, published as *School of the Sun*, 1960]); others rebel against the destruction of their principles: several young protagonists react against the war in *En esta tierra* (In this land, 1955), while *Los soldados lloran de noche* (The soldiers cry in the night, 1964) ends with a gratuitous self-sacrifice. Even younger writers like Ana María Moix (b. 1947) begin their careers with very personal chronicles of disillusionment; *Julia* (1969) traces the progressive psychological alienation of a young child whose rejection takes the form of psychological withdrawal.[2]

Although the adolescent is an effective symbol of loss of innocence, many adults in these novels also have symbolic roles. Generally they are cast as victims—of society, of a specific historical event, of an unhappy relationship, but most often as victims of their own personal obsessions, problems, or attitudes. Disillusionment often characterizes their outlook, and their abulia and apathy result from the realization that they are almost powerless in the face of overwhelming pressures. Many of Ignacio Aldecoa's best novels develop an individual's attitudes and behavior under great stress (or limit-situations)—a fugitive from justice in *Con el viento solano* (With the east wind, 1956) or the confrontation of antithetical life-styles transcending social framework in *Parte de una historia* (Part of a story, 1967).

The Civil War becomes a focal point in many of the works of subjective neorealism, although these novelists do not write war novels in the true sense of the word. Nevertheless, the results of the holocaust, emotional as well as political and economic, the predicament of those who did not win, their subsequent ostracism or mistreatment, and the loss of friends, family, and particularly of ideals for which one has struggled form a personal history that appears time and again in the works of the Mid-Century Generation. In their eyes, the conflict transcends its historical importance to become a paradigm of other conflicts, age-old and apparently inevitable. One of the most poignant treatments of this attitude appears in Ana María Matute's *Los hijos muertos* (Dead children, published as *The Lost Children*, 1958) a complex work of interwoven time frames, fragmentation, interior and exterior perspectives. One of the protagonists, now a broken, disillusioned man, remembers former relationships, the Civil War, and its tragic consequences and prefers to live as a hermit because of all of these things.[3]

As the emphasis in these works is on the individual, the state of mind of that character becomes more instrumental in setting the tone of the novel. In most cases, the protagonists are misfits in a place and time to which they cannot adjust. Anguish, pessimism, alienation, disappointment, and despair follow these characters, whose solitude is apparent even in the company of friends and family. Lack of communication is a constant leitmotif: the characters are unable or unwilling to share their concerns with others. If they do attempt to break through the wall of indifference, the result is misunderstanding, suspicion, or hostility.

The disillusionment characteristic of most adult protagonists often causes a search into the past, whether for an analysis of the roots of the problem or for comfort in the remembrance of happier, more carefree days. The theme of return or remembrance thus structures a large number of these works. Several of Elena Quiroga's psychological novels move along the lines of remembrance, creating an investigation into the past from a more recent perspective. Matute's *Los hijos muertos, Primera memoria, La trampa* (The trap, 1969), and an excellent short novel, *Fiesta al noroeste* (Celebration in the Northwest, 1952) use this perspective; Ana María Moix's *Walter ¿por qué te fuiste?* (Walter, why did you leave?, 1973) combines the quest theme with the return to childhood. In the course of the novel, the reader discovers—often piecemeal—hidden circumstances known only to the one who recollects. The contrast of past and present heightens emotional undercurrents, and the sense of loss may make the present almost intolerable.

The use of the past to explain or justify the present enhances the intensely personal focus of subjective neorealism: it emphasizes the individual's preeminence in that a personal conception of reality also embraces historical fact. The distortion or reinterpretation of certain facts may be explained by the intervening time between fact and narration or the distance separating subject and object of narration (which may often be simply the younger double of the speaker). In *La oscura historia de la prima Montse* (The hidden story of Cousin Montse, 1970), Juan Marsé not only involves his reader in temporal distancing (chronological separation) in his attack on bourgeois values and behavior, but in spatial (exile) and narrative distancing (ironic stance) as well.

The novelists mold the subject of time into a theme as well as a structural determinant, so that it transcends its complementary function to become the topic of the work. The simple present becomes a springboard for an investigation into the complex nature of time. The subject of return to a lost past appears in many guises: the past as a refuge (the prelapsarian innocence of childhood), as paradigm (parallels of behavior suggesting unchanging nature), as contrast (innocence and naiveté pitted against adult apathy), or as part of situational reality (personal, regional, or national history). In the psychological novel or in those works contrasting inner and outer reality, present time is deliberately swelled with the insertion of the past, which may surge up through association or through the more technical means of interior monologue or stream of consciousness.

The introduction of dual temporal planes (which may be clearly apparent or inferred through symbols) is one example of experimentation with the subject. The author establishes a paradigm or referential situation that clearly links the behavior or emotion with an archetypal pattern, thus expanding the limits of the work considerably without necessity of explicit authorial "message." Mythic or archetypal figures suggest infinite possibilities (the scapegoat, Prometheus); biblical patterns inform some of the works (Peter's betrayal in *Primera memoria,* Cain and Abel in *Duelo en el Paraíso*). Paradise lost appears in several of the Goytisolo's novels,[4] as do classical references (Proteus, Icarus, Medea). Inevitable changes through rites of passage, the use of interior time and space (either through the remembrances of the character or the paradigms mentioned above), or the fusion of two different ages through human constants offer commentaries that transcend the plot of the work.

The subjective neorealists decompose experience into fragments, rearranged according to emotional, not chronological, time. This explains the heavy reliance on the interior monologue characterizing so many of these works. The psychological approach reveals the inner world of the characters, whose thoughts surge up from their unconscious, summoned by a word, an object, or a similar emotion, binding two or more time frames together. Several novelists attempt to merge past and present through parenthetical insertions, italics, or other typographical indications that create the illusion of simultaneity. The introduction of the leitmotif or symbol is particularly apt in this case, because once he establishes the special meaning of an element, the writer can rely on it for affective values without the need of further explanation on the conscious level (Matute's use of water or fairy tales in *Primera memoria,* for example). The influence of the cinema is also evident in the use of juxtaposition and montage, transferred to literature in the associative thought or word patterns, the insertion of running commentaries within the novel's action, and the attempt to provide both inner and outer dimensions simultaneously. For example, the widow in Delibes's *Cinco horas con Mario* (Five hours with Mario, 1966) begins to read a passage from the Bible but immediately drifts off into more mundane thoughts that unconsciously arise from the words.

Both objective and social neorealism require detailed, objective descriptions; inner reality requires an entirely different approach. For this reason, a decidedly experimental vein characterizes the techniques of subjective neorealism. In addition to the efforts to meld form and content by meshing different time frames and psychological states of mind (leitmotifs, montage, interior monologue), there is a marked interest in aesthetic effects as communicative devices between author and reader. Metaphor, simile, lyrical passages, accumulation, reiteration, and many other devices allow the artistic dimension to transmit the emotions and reactions of author or character without the necessity of direct intervention. Strange metaphors create a feeling of anxiety; a heavily lyrical style often appeals to the emotions or senses as a type of subliminal means of conveying impressions. These affective techniques bind the reader closely to the character, since he can only perceive reality through the character's limited field of vision. Although the author may not state directly that the character feels threatened, anxious, or unhappy, two or three well-placed parenthetical thoughts, the suggestion of a leitmotif associated with some decisive past event, or an unusual metaphor may convey with greater force the type of emotional reaction directly experienced. For example, Matute's *Fiesta al noroeste* opens as Dingo draws near Artámila, scene of his unhappy childhood. The sky and land appear hostile to man;[5] the road is "precipitous and violent, there only to swallow one up" (10); the sky is "implacable" (11), the rain "indifferent" (13). The personification alone would support the change in relationship between the man and the usually passive background of nature; the malevolent attributes reinforce Dingo's apprehensions and set the scene for the forthcoming tragedy.[6] The violence of both language and situation linked to the mirror motif in Cela's *Vísperas, festividad y octava de San Camilo del año 1936 en Madrid* (Vespers, celebration and octave of Saint Camilo in the year 1936 in Madrid, 1969) imparts the same effect on both psychological and historical levels. These and other literary techniques suggest an expressionistic aesthetic of distortion, which simultaneously justifies and reinforces the unique point of view.

The aesthetics of distortion offer a particularly effective complement for the psychological novel. In contrast with those works which elaborate surface phenomena, the psychological novel explores the inner dimension, the development of a personality, or the effect of certain experiences on an unusually sensitive individual. Solitude, lack of communication, unhappiness, or a sense of estrangement often characterizes these people, whose introversion leads to intensive self-analysis. The novels of Elena Quiroga, for example, combine different time frames and perspectives in their exploration of inner thoughts: *Algo pasa en la calle* (Something is happening in the street, 1954) and *La enferma* (The invalid, 1955) reveal the life of a person through thoughts and memories of others; *Tristura* (Sadness, 1960) and *Escribo tu nombre* (I write your name, 1965) trace the development and experiences of young Tadea.

The exploration of the psychological dimension is one of the most characteristic notes of Ramón Hernández. His works analyze the intimate world of a single or of several characters who find themselves in an existential situation requiring reevaluation of the past and a decision to direct their lives. His *Palabras en el muro* (Words on the wall, 1969) traces the intermingling thoughts of three prisoners in a cell. *Ira en la noche* (Rage in the night, 1970) explores madness; *El tirano inmóvil* (The unmovable tyrant, 1970) pits man against oppressive forces; *Eterna memoria* (Eternal memory, 1975) poses war as a metaphor for modern man's problems, his quest for identity, his feelings of guilt, and the absurdity of life. Hernández's experimental tendencies and his heavy use of symbols and allegorical elements place him on the fringe of realistic practices, although his interest in man and his place in society never removes him completely from the concerns of the neorealists.

Elena Soriano's trilogy *Mujer y hombre* (Woman and man, 1955) uses sexual love for its existential as well as its erotic aspects. *La playa de los locos* (The beach of madmen), *Espejismos* (Mirages), and *Medea 55* delve into the relationship between the sexes, problems of communication, and the necessity for decision. The exploration of the inner world of her characters (through flashback and analysis) goes beyond the psychological novel to suggest a more intellectual preoccupation.

Antonio Martínez-Menchen's *Cinco variaciones* (Five variations, 1963), with its musical implications, comprises five cases of loneliness in ordinary people of varying ages and in different settings (for example, a man who attends a class reunion and feels his solitude and alienation in the midst of the merrymaking; a student who follows a girl through the city, thinking about love and the loss of his mother). Miguel Delibes's *Cinco horas con Mario* takes place almost exclusively within the mind of a single character, but the inner space and time that fill her memories expand the scope of the novel to include both personal and historical dimensions.

Ignacio Aldecoa is one of the finest writers of the Mid-Century Generation. Although many of his works reveal social concerns, particularly because of the professional slant (the rural policeman in *El fulgor y la sangre* [Lightning and blood, 1954) or fishing in *Gran sol* [Great Sole, 1957]), Aldecoa differs from the social neorealists in his passion for stylistic excellence, his habit of placing his characters in situations that transcend national problems, and his use of paradigms, archetypes, and other patterns that suggest universal human behavior. His last work, *Parte de una historia* (Part of a story, 1967), blends personal, social, and universal aspects in the confrontation of two antithetical ways of life.

Carmen Martín Gaite's works have delved into the problems of adjustment between personal aspirations and expectations imposed by society from without. From the more social focus of *Entre visillos,* she moves to an individual's alienation in *Ritmo lento* (Slow rhythm, 1962) and refines the personal, introspective viewpoint in *Retahilas* (Threads of discourse, 1974), in which a night of dialogue between two people brings their common backgrounds and present feelings into focus, affirming their own direction through words and memory. Observations on the nature of language and communication enrich the personal story, which in turn transcends its purely anecdotal function.

Two novels with plots similar to those of the social novel illustrate the difference in perspective between it and subjectivist works. *Ultimas tardes con Teresa* (Final afternoons with Teresa, 1966), by Juan Marsé, and García Hortelano's *El gran momento de Mary Tribune* (Mary Tribune's great moment, 1972) both have protagonists who could be considered as group representatives, explore contacts between different social groups, and offer an indictment of the middle class. But instead of describing the situation impassively, each author selects a multidimensional approach that includes his own undisguised point of view, conveyed through a number of stylistic and situational means. *Ultimas tardes* chronicles the meeting between a rich young lady (Teresa) and a lower-class boy with aspirations to a better life (Pijoaparte). A host of secondary characters reinforces the social typology (ineffectual leftist students versus the inhabitants of Pijoaparte's world). Pijoaparte's efforts to enter into more exalted spheres begins with his conquest of a girl he mistakes for Teresa but who actually is the maid. The boy's fantasies (that he is the son of a marquis, or that he rescues Teresa from danger) are ludicrous. Deliberate incongruity is one of the trademarks of the work, supported by intertextual references that only magnify the distance between reality and fantasy. Marsé himself intervenes to offer opinions, and even allows himself to be mentioned in the text as a writer. One critic suggests that *Ultimas tardes* is actually a parody of the social novel, particularly in the latter's denunciation of bourgeois decadence and its concern for the suffering of the lower classes: "The bitter and small *Quijote* of the social narrative, this book is, in itself, an excellent social novel in the way that the *Quijote* was the best possible book of chivalry, . . . no longer objective, but rather . . . indirect, subjective, expansive, satirical, angry."[7] Because of these elements critics have noted the influence of Martín-Santos's *Tiempo de silencio,* published four years previously.

In *El gran momento de Mary Tribune,* an ambitious two-volume study of bourgeois life, García Hortelano analyzes the same behavior patterns and environment as in his earlier novels, but with a notable change in perspective: the first-person narrator, the humor, exaggeration, and irony of situation, and experimentation with various time frames pursue a different view of reality symbolized by the narrator himself, who affords a dual vision of his class through his simultaneous participation in and alienation from what he describes. García Hortelano expands the linguistic dimension of the work by the invention of new words or the recombination of common ones, and by the inclusion of an amazing variety of speech, slang, dialect, and jargon representing social, professional, and geographical peculiarities. The addition of humor (in caricature, sarcasm, or incongruous situations) and the intertextual references to literature, art, and cinema make the reader aware of a rather self-conscious work. The creation of a reality that transcends (and perhaps explains) the present situation goes far beyond the intentions of neorealism. The linguistic and cultural additions, as well as the stance of the author, place *El gran momento* in the tradition of *Tiempo de silencio;* at the very least, the work stands at the threshold of the New Novel, in an evolution that removes García Hortelano from the concerns of neorealism he had earlier espoused.

Paralleling the neorealistic movement is the "Metaphysical Group," so called for the obvious reason that the writers' interests transcend the concerns of contemporary reality and particularly because there is an absence of the same critical intention that characterizes the works of their fellow novelists. Art is now placed at the service of values, ideas, religion, or philosophical issues rather than social analysis. Several of the "metaphysical" works are clearly allegorical, with minimal connections to contemporary reality. Some deal with the individual in his dual role of citizen of his times and representative of the idea that the author develops. Certain critics have dealt harshly with the group as a whole, intimating that the preeminence of the "idea" has resulted in a less rounded work (schematic characters, implausibility of situation, etc.).

The chief defender and spokesman for this type of literature (and specifically for the Metaphysical Group, which he himself named) is critic and novelist M. García Viñó. In one study, after reviewing critical analyses of social literature, he concludes that "we have never seen any of these others [writers'] names who . . . are every bit as social and realistic as the first group, and, in some cases, somewhat better writers: [Julio] Manegat, [Victor] Alperi, [Jorge] Ferrer-Vidal, [Juan] Molla, [Francisco] Candel, [José María] Castillo-Navarro, [José Luis] Martín Descalzo, perhaps because social and documentary realism in these cases, has a third name, whether it be *transcendent, Catholic, poetic,* or even *personal.*"[8] To this list he later adds Antonio Prieto, Carlos Rojas, Andrés Bosch, Claudio Bassols, Iñigo de Aranzadi, José Tomás Cabot, Pedro Sánchez Paredes, Juan Bonet, Miguel Buñuel, José Vidals Cadellans, Manuel San Martín, and himself, offering a thematic division with illustrative titles (exoticism, utopia, poetry, super- or infrareality, symbolism, and metaphysical and theological problems) concerning which he insists that ". . . although the goals that determine them are of a metaphysical and aesthetic disposition, the fact is that most of them encompass, in a wider dimension, that world and that time [in which the authors live]" (66–68).

This list might also include individual works of older writers not directly connected with the Metaphysical Group. The "Catholic novel," or at least those works that develop religious questions, would include Carmen Laforet's *La mujer nueva* (The new woman, 1955), which feminizes St. Paul's words to suit the case of a contemporary woman who reaffirms her faith, or José Luis Castillo-Puche's *Sin camino* (Without direction, 1956), which concerns priesthood as a vocational choice. Castillo-Puche has also described an existential posture in the face of an uncertain and frightening world: *Con la muerte al hombro* (With death at my shoulder, 1954) presents the morbid fear of death and the varying ways in which one faces the unknown.[9] One could also include Gonzalo Torrente Ballester, whose first works analyze man in his human and mythic dimensions.

His trilogy *Los gozos y las sombras,* composed of *El Señor llega* (The Master comes, 1957), *Donde da la vuelta el aire* (Where the air turns, 1960), and *La Pascua triste* (Sad Easter, 1962), opposes two individuals representing different ideologies; the implications are symbolic as well as psychological. Torrente Ballester's later works, involving myth and incursions into the fantastic (for example, *Don Juan,* 1963), ally him to more and more with the New Novel.

Despite the fact that the Mid-Century Generation had access to the same international influences, the subjective neorealists not only adapted those that most affected their objective counterparts (Italian neorealism, cinema, American Lost Generation) but added to them an interest in Joyce, Proust, and Kafka; some of the literature of the absurd; American writers such as Truman Capote, Carson McCullers, and William Styron; Freudian and Jungian psychology; existential writers; and Bergsonian philosophy.

The subjective novelists managed to combine the best of neorealism with the human dimension to produce more artistic and transcendent works. These writers, in general, have survived the negative criticism leveled at the objectivist and social novelists. It seems that they have discovered a formula that translates both contemporary and universal concerns into a single work that, by some means, strikes an answering chord in the reader, who finds validity on many levels. From the subjective perspective of these writers, it was not a great step to the more radically experimental literature of the later period; its techniques provided stepping stones for many of these same writers to the later, more abstract (but no less personal) mode.

Primera memoria

Ana María Matute is a member of the Mid-Century Generation, but her interests go far beyond the thematics of social relations and group dynamics found in the works of her contemporaries. Even though she still actively writes, hers is a body of literature that already presents a clearly defined philosophy of life, varying only in the form in which she presents it. Her trilogy *Los mercaderes* (The moneychangers) is an indictment of materialists who refuse to acknowledge their responsibility toward those less fortunate. Thus, while elements common to the social novel are apparent, more important are the universal constants that give her works their atemporal quality. Of the three novels, the first—*Primera memoria* (Early Memories, published as *School of the Sun*)—which won the 1959 Nadal prize, is a most appropriate example of subjective realism.

The plot revolves around Matia, who recounts a painful—and symbolic—episode in her childhood. The episode takes place on an island (supposedly Mallorca, but never specified in the novel) during the Civil War, where young Matia lives while her widowed father is fighting in the war. There she, her male cousin Borja, and Borja's mother, Emilia, live with her domineering grandmother, whose powerful social and economic position makes her an object of respect and fear on the island. Matia and Borja have a number of escapades together, including "fights" between their group of friends and a rival group, but eventually Manuel Taronjí enters the scene and inspires, unwittingly, a jealous reaction in Borja, both because of Matia's preference for Manuel and, worse, because Borja discovers that Manuel is the illegitimate son of an idolized relative, Jorge de Son Major. Borja falsely accuses Manuel of having stolen money, and Matia, given the opportunity to tell the truth and vindicate her friend, remains silent out of cowardice. Manuel is sent to reform school; Borja and Matia are left with their dishonesty and betrayal, respectively.

A novel of such richness lends itself to many analytical approaches. Certain thematic preoccupations of social realism are present: the obvious and well-guarded class division, seen throughout the book in the grandmother's attitude toward her "inferiors," her social expectations for the grandchildren, the behavior of her peers, and their interactions at social gatherings. A further "division" is set up in political terms, while the Civil War is raging on the mainland—and ever-present through allusions on the island—we are reminded about the seriousness of the division through the political assassinations on the island (one of whom is Manuel's adoptive father), the ostracism and harassment accorded to families on the wrong side, and the fact that the fathers of Matia and Borja are fighting on opposite sides.

On a universal plane, however, the indictments become more general in nature. Cruelty, fear, hypocrisy, false charity, pretentiousness, gross materialism, and egoism characterize the majority of the inhabitants on an island that is doubtless a microcosm of a larger system. Prejudice and distrust are common and perpetuated carefully down through the generations; cases of real or disinterested affection are doomed (Matia betrays Manuel; the one case of true affection—the servant Antonia and her son Lauro—is destroyed by the latter's death, of which the reader learns later).

Since the novel is about adolescents, not adults, their behavior may not be as much imitative as preordained. In other words, Matute displays a critical view of reality, but it transcends the historical movement. Early on, she establishes a cyclic view of time: "Could it be true that as children we live our whole lives, in one gulp, only to repeat ourselves afterwards stupidly, blindly, without any sense?"[10] The symbolism of the young characters is thus crucial to the message. They may lack the historicopolitical experience to comprehend the reasons for the opposition, but naturally fall into paradigms that suggest a continual and inevitable repetition of a single event, and as such their function is metonymic. While the assassinations and rigid class divisions point to an ideological struggle, the children's wars between the "haves" and "have-nots" echo this struggle on another level (94 ff.). Significantly, they take place on the plaza where many centuries ago prejudice and ill-will were responsible for the burning of the Mallorcan Jews. This is only one example of Matute's use of historical strata to underscore her point. A biblical parallel also suggests unalterable patterns of human degeneration: the betrayal of Christ reenacted in Borja's (i.e., Judas's) accusation of Manuel (Christ) and Matia's (Peter's) cowardly denial of him the traditional three times. The Cain-Abel theme, another constant in Matute's work, appears with variations in the love-hate relationship of Manuel and Borja (who aspires to be Jorge's son) and in the view of the Civil War as fratricide.

The amalgamation of narrative voices, dominated by the older Matia's parenthetical comments, dialogue, and references to past events, makes it difficult to distinguish clearly the various time frames (a narrative technique that obviously complements the themes mentioned above). However, these voices also provide a chronicle of the maturation of a young girl to womanhood, a process against which she desperately and futilely rebels. Examples everywhere convince her that she wants nothing of the adult world, but as inevitably as brother fights brother, or Peter betrays Christ, an unwritten law—this time biological—defeats her intentions: "I was about to grow and become a woman. . . . 'No, no, wait a little longer . . . a little longer.' But, who had to wait? I was the one, only I, who was betraying myself each instant" (148). Matia's betrayal of Manuel is also a betrayal of the idealism of her childhood, and she enters adulthood through this rite of passage. The use of role models (her aunt and grandmother) as images of the future completes the horrible but inexorable fate awaiting her.

Stylistic techniques emphasize the subjective nature of this novel. The viewpoint is restricted exclusively to the older Matia, who colors the past with a hopelessness that the reader experiences as well. Leitmotifs, rhetorical devices, and lyrical, metaphorical passages are designed specifically to arouse emotional rather than intellectual reactions; a series of images evokes Matia's happier childhood, which is doomed to disappear (fairy tales, water, a toy puppet theater, apples from her former home); these images appear in times of great stress, subtly indicating the hidden desire to escape from present reality and return to childhood. Constant references to nature in its personalized and threatening capacity suggest instability and surprise: "The sun cut across the transparent skin of the sky like a swollen burn" (209). People are dehumanized, objects personified. One of the most chilling examples of the unusual and threatening role of objects appears in Matia's impressions of the bathroom: "The bathtub . . . had great, black marks, like stigmata of an evil race. On the walls stood out spots of rust and moisture forming strange continents, tears of old age and abandonment" (73). The pessimism that characterizes many of the works of this period finds poignant expression in the novels of Ana María Matute, especially in *Primera memoria*. Her originality and unusual modes of expression have given her a place of importance in the Mid-Century Generation.[11]

Cinco horas con Mario

Miguel Delibes's continuous literary output has not been associated with a single movement, but his thematic constant—man and his relationship with his historical circumstances—has undergone interesting formal changes that roughly follow the evolution of the Spanish novel analyzed in this book. *Cinco horas con Mario* (Five hours with Mario, 1966) typifies work of the later period of subjective neorealism; its innovative techniques and unusual subject matter place it in an important pivotal position, allying it in some ways with *Tiempo de silencio* of Martín-Santos (1962) and pointing to newer interpretations that characterize the Spanish New Novel.[12]

The five hours in the title refer to the time the recently widowed Carmen sits next to the coffin of her husband, reading the Bible.

The limited time and space expand through recollection as Carmen reconstructs their life together. Since the action takes place almost exclusively in memory, this work falls partially within the techniques of the psychological novel. Through a continuous interior monologue, Carmen discloses her true personality: she is petty, selfish, uncharitable, and hypocritical. It is obvious that she and Mario were not really suited for each other, and that a lack of communication and a good measure of bad faith marred their relationship.

Three motifs structure Carmen's view of life: money, sex, and ideological differences. She is annoyed that Mario's principles would not allow him to follow her advice to write cheap novels, which would make money; she is ashamed because she cannot keep up with her friends (she mentions the long-desired car so much that it becomes a symbol of her pretensions and Mario's "failures"); she is utterly insensitive concerning her sexual relationship with Mario (she refuses to believe that he was not sexually experienced when they wed; she never forgives him for not consummating their marriage on their wedding night; she accuses him of affairs). They never seem to have agreed on anything: he is liberal, concerned with human rights and intellectual matters; she is conservative, rigid and selfish. Even their families and ideologies are not compatible: they represented opposing sides in the Civil War. Somewhat in the manner of a detective novel, the self-revelations probe ever deeper until they reveal the secret (hidden almost from herself) that she was unfaithful to Mario in spirit if not in fact. This terrible moment represents possibly the only authentic act in her life, and quickly passes when she dons her "social mask" as another person enters the room.

Delibes has achieved masterful effects in *Cinco horas*. Except for the brief prologue and epilogue, the novel is completely character-dominated. Carmen speaks in a "dialogue" with Mario, using the second-person-familiar form, which is, in effect, a monologue. Thus the character reveals herself without interference from the author, and the reader is drawn into her world of values, focused through her thoughts. It is not necessary for Delibes to offer judgments; Carmen presents the damning evidence herself. Her thoughts are actually a list of complaints concerning Mario's ineptitude, mistakes, and ingratitude, and, by contrast or implication, her own innocence and miscomprehension. One of the ironies of the work is that Carmen's accusations against Mario actually turn against her: despite the fact that Mario cannot defend himself, the "objective" material is evidence enough to condemn Carmen the woman, as well as the system for which she stands. Delibes criticizes not only the middle class, but a Spanish way of life. The opposing ideologies may well symbolize abstractions beyond the actual marriage: the uneasy marriage of opposing political views in Spain. There is obvious condemnation of the conservative, bourgeois value system, which transcends narrow political matters to embrace an entire worldview and resultant behavior.

Carmen's thoughts are responsible for the minimal plot in the novel; the manner in which she expresses herself reveals more about her way of life than the content itself. Each of the chapters begins with a selection from the Bible. Choosing those passages that Mario had underlined (cleverly indicating his interests and way of life), Carmen reads them to herself. But she cannot (or will not) take the words at face value; instead, she construes the meaning through a highly personal interpretation, disclosing the selfish attitudes that obviously have structured their relationship together. A typical example begins chapter 5: *"Come and see the works of Yaveh, the wonders that he has wrought over the land. He is the one who makes war cease unto the ends of the earth. He breaks the bow, shatters the lance and makes the shields burn in the fire,* although whatever you may say, I did have a good time during the war, you know, I don't know if I am too frivolous or whatever, but I spent some fabulous years, the best of my life, you know, everyone as if on vacation, the street full of boys, and all that uproar" (73). As usual, she interprets the words to suit her own point of view (that is, directed only toward her feelings and reactions), not allowing them their original value.

Delibes's skill with language, one of his literary fortes, rises to a new peak in *Cinco horas*.[13] The biblical phrases contrast sharply with the colloquial speech of Carmen, peppered with interjections, slang and popular expressions, commonplaces, stock phrases, proverbs, and sayings, indicating a prosaic and imitative mind. Such pedestrian language reveals that Carmen's entire world is composed of limited *idées fixes*, traditional notions that come from class conditioning rather than reflective thought. She is outwardly religious, and defends modesty and woman's place in the home, proper behavior, the reasons for keeping up appearances. These values appear time and again in her thoughts on behavior: "As far as I'm concerned, anything rather than let your manners go . . . at home they really drilled it into me, now you see" (61); on Spain's place in the world: "We must defend what is ours" (77), or a quotation from one of her father's articles, which ends, "perhaps we don't have machines, but we do have spiritual values and decency to export" (78); on woman's role in life: schooling is of little value (75); her mother said that books were good only to put on one's head to improve posture (76); on government: "A strong authority is the guarantee of order" (135); and so on.

Despite the fact that the novel is essentially composed of inner movement, it is solidly grounded in the reality that underlies it. Carmen represents the middle class, but even more she typifies an attitude prevalent at the time the book was written, a fact noted by several critics. [14] Delibes stands well within the tradition of neo-realism by virtue of his criticism of specific social structures, attitudes, and upbringing in contemporary Spain. Nevertheless, the novel transcends objective criticism of contemporary conditions. The ironical overlay apparent in the contradictory evidence, [15] the restrictive focus used as revelatory agent, and the use of language to reveal attitude as well as plot are features that make *Cinco horas* a very personal chronicle of the unhappiness and alienation of an individual at odds with the milieu (a fact that applies to Carmen as well as Mario). The reliance on the character for self-preservation creates a reader-directed text, which, along with the interest in language as revelatory and central agent, points to concerns of the New Novel, a direction Delibes takes in this and, more fully, in later works. [16]

Chapter Eight
Tiempo de silencio

To understand the unique place of *Tiempo de silencio* (*Time of Silence*) in contemporary Spanish literature, one must place it within the historical perspective of 1962, the year of publication.[1] Basic forms of realism still dominated the literary scene, although there were variations on that mode: the popular traditional, Galdosian-inspired novels, the contemporary social focus, and more subjective interpretations of contemporary reality with emphasis on inner character development. Finally, a small number of writers formed part of a more intellectual group, which never espoused the tenets of neorealism.

With little national tradition to prepare readers for the publication of a work of such radical departure from traditional norms, reactions were mixed. Everything about *Tiempo de silencio* was extreme: the personal, subjective tone, the language, the multiple points of view, experimentation in tone and styles, bitter criticism of national as well as social issues. Its critical reception, predictably, was not uniformly enthusiastic.[2] Nevertheless, many immediately recognized the unique character of the novel and its place as pioneer in a new literature: it was called "unrepeatable and unimitable."[3] The recognition that its author, Luis Martín-Santos, deserved came largely after his untimely death in 1964, and includes, to date, well over fifty studies of the work itself, in addition to countless references to the novel's historical and literary place in Spanish letters.

Linear plot summary cannot do justice to the complex nature of *Tiempo,* since plot as such is only a single thread holding together a rich and intricate amalgamation of form and content. Pedro, a young scientist, dreams of winning the Nobel prize by achieving a breakthrough in his research, which he hopes will prove that cancer is transmitted by a virus rather than by heredity or chance. This in turn would imply that a cure might be possible in the form of a vaccine. As the novel opens, Pedro is lamenting the death of his last experimental mouse and the lack of funds for obtaining a fresh supply. His assistant, Amador, offers to get him more: his cousin

Muecas, previously fired from the institute for stealing and reselling used test animals, has been secretly breeding this special strain in his shack. Amador leads Pedro to the slum of *chabolas* and reveals a world hitherto unknown to him: a life of abject poverty and misery, where the standard of living falls far below that of primitives in other parts of the world, in which the houses are constructed out of orange crates and tin cans, where an entire family shares a bed and lives on garbage and cast-offs from Madrid. Muecas attributes his success in breeding mice to his unique system: his daughters carry the animals in their breasts to keep them warm and induce them to go into heat. Florita even complains that the mice are so lively that they bite her.

From there, Pedro returns to an entirely different environment: the world of the middle-class *pension* where he has rented a room. The three women who run the *pension* (the lovely Dorita, her mother, and grandmother) have designs on Pedro as a good match for Dorita. That evening, Pedro and his wealthy friend Matias go on a drinking spree and visit a house of prostitution. He returns home drunk, thinking of sex, and enters Dorita's room, where he is received with a warm "my love." Vaguely realizing that he is now trapped, he goes back to bed, only to be awakened by a desperate Amador, who incoherently babbles that Florita needs his help. Remembering the mouse bites and assuming that his theory of viral cancer can now be proven, Pedro rushes to her side, only to find her dying from a botched abortion; Muecas is the "father-grandfather" (107). Pedro further implicates himself by completing the abortion although he is not licensed to practice medicine, and, realizing that the girl is dead, he rushes out into the night to hide in the house of prostitution instead of reporting the facts to the police. There he is caught, jailed, and finally exonerated by the girl's mother. Thoroughly chastened, he decides to settle down to a life of bourgeois mediocrity: he dutifully attends the engagement party at the *pension,* accepts the fact that he can no longer continue at the institute because of the scandal in which he was involved (he will take his examinations and become a country doctor), and finally escorts the mother and fiancée to a fair, where Dorita is killed by Florita's vengeful boyfriend Cartucho, wrongly informed as to Pedro's role in the girl's death. Pedro leaves for the country, acknowledging the end of his hopes, coinciding with a personal and national "time of silence."

The brief chronological adventure in Pedro's life is simply one part of a fragmentary narration enriched with a large number of episodes that may or may not bear directly on the *histoire,* so that ostensibly individual scenes expand to encompass social, national, and universal concerns. One critic has tied the new type of writing to the changing economic levels of Spain: ". . . as development is effected, the theme that is posed to the novelist is not the denunciation of facts, but the attempt to conceive the global sense of society."[4]

Martín-Santos was certainly cognizant of his fresh approach to the novel, and, in the few opportunities available to express his theory of literature, elaborated his idea of dialectical realism, which, in contrast to the static description of alienation that characterizes the social novel, establishes a constant and dynamic conflict.[5] He distinguishes three prevalent types of realism in the twentieth-century Spanish novel: realism of the Generation of 1898; a neopicaresque or *pueblerino* realism (presenting individuals who are ahistorical but uniquely Spanish in character, like the *pícaro*), and *suburbano* realism (which concentrates on generic types, exemplifies historical determinism, and offers practical examples of social theories). His awareness and criticism of the pitfalls of both social and objectivist novels led him to select a different approach, one that acknowledges the existence of a multifaceted reality and stylistically conveys that reality to the reader. From this literary viewpoint emerges the *"monólogo dialéctico,"* which, as Martín-Santos explains in an interview, allows a double plane of reality to be present simultaneously: the sequential narrative of an episode along with an interior monologue providing the character's commentary, reaction, and feelings on an internal level.[6] From this point of departure, it is not difficult to construct a theory of dialectical realism pitting one element against another, offering a dynamic conflict and movement toward change or resolution, while portraying a synchronic conception of reality. Broadly speaking, the major elements that come into conflict are individual, social, and national, with endless variations of each in interplay. To elaborate on these elements, Martín-Santos relies partially on the tradition of the social novel while at the same time creating an entirely new approach in the complex interrelationship of character-reader-author.

Several obvious aspects link *Tiempo de silencio* with prevailing themes of neorealism, the major one being the constant awareness of class and type, which form the basis of Spanish society. The critical function of the work is another link with neorealism: the novelist's avowed purpose is to use literature to reveal the "truth" during an era when censorship was prevalent.[7] Thus the reader perceives the misery of the slum dwellers, the lack of interest among the various social classes, the ambience of the city, which, in a general way, symbolizes a type of environmental as well as social determinism. In addition to the dissection of the conventional class divisions (upper, middle, and lower), Martín-Santos delves further into the special taxonomy of subgroups: the intellectual crowd of painters and writers, the house of prostitution, the hierarchies at the institute, the bureaucracy of legal and penal systems. Martín-Santos enriches *Tiempo de silencio* with an undisguisedly subjective point of view: shifting styles, multiple perspectives, and an intellectually conceived work make his point of view obvious to the reader, while at the same time creating a deliberate aesthetic distance to prevent identification with any of the characters. One point of intersection with neorealism—criticism of contemporary Spanish conditions and the misery of the lower classes—provides a clear example of how the same subject can evoke such a divergent response.

The *chabola* world is one of abject poverty and subhuman standards. This terrible condition had already been seized as a point of criticism by several social novelists, among them Antonio Ferres *(La piqueta)*, García Hortelano *(Nuevas amistades)*, or Angel María de Lera *(Los olvidados)*. Each describes the physical and mental isolation characteristic of this place and offers grim details that document the subhuman level of existence. Martín-Santos, however, leads the reader beyond the objectively presented picture, making use of parody, incongruity, and irony to express the indignation and horror evoked by the scene. He begins with a mock-epic style, a parodic form particularly appropriate for the incongruous, sarcastic tone to follow: "With what happy hopes the two fellow workers embarked on their journey toward the legendary *chabolas* and Muecas's rabbit- and mouse-breeding grounds" (25). Nearing the settlement, Pedro espies some miserable-looking shacks with burlap covering the entrances. Asking Amador if those are the *chabolas,* he receives the following reply: "Those? . . . No, those are houses" (32). Thus establishing the unimaginable squalor in which these people live, Martín-Santos ushers in the description of the miserable place with literary fanfare—"There were the chabolas!" (42)—and precedes a detailed enumerative description of the wretched existence that they lead with the ironic oxymoron characterizing them as "proud fortresses of misery" (42).

Pedro's arrival at Muecas's dwelling precipitates a new approach: the complete inversion of reality through descriptive presentation. The hovel becomes a fine ranch and Muecas's illegal mouse-producing business is transformed into a thoroughbred horse-breeding industry (56 ff.). Martín-Santos provides further indications of the unbelievable conditions in which this family lives with a tongue-in-cheek, pseudoscientific anthropological comparison with life among the primitives, in which the latter fare better than these miserable "modern" citizens. Why go to far-off places to study human behavior, asks the narrator: "As if it had not been shown that in the interior of an Eskimo igloo the temperature in January is several degrees Fahrenheit above that in the Madrid *chabola*. As if one didn't know that the mean age for loss of virginity is lower in these hovels than in the tribes of Central Africa, which are endowed with such complex and grotesque initiation rites" (44).

The middle class fares no better. The novelist selects still another viewpoint from which to expose problems of the bourgeoisie, significantly represented only by women. The grandmother presents her family history in a rambling monologue, describing her husband, who contracted a venereal disease during the campaigns in the Philippines, and her mannish daughter, from whose effeminate husband Dorita inherited her graceful manner. Left with a minimal government pension, the grandmother genteelly pimps for her daughter to get enough capital for the pseudorespectability of a *pension*, where she keeps a vigilant eye on the pursestrings. References to menopause and alcoholism only underline the monotony and hopelessness of her situation. All hopes for the future rest on the granddaughter's success in marrying a promising young man.

Matias's mother and friends represent the upper class, who meet in her apartment to attend a reception for the famous philosopher Ortega y Gasset (never named as such, but allusions clearly point to him). A cleverly sustained metaphor comparing the guests to birds (135 ff.) transmits the unsubstantial, flighty nature of the gathering.

Pedro provides the only contact among these very separate beings. Since each class is equal in its passivity and narrowness of vision, one can only assume that the problem is of national scope. The inability to transcend personal interest, and the reactions in the face of trouble, the refusal to help one another or to cross professional or social boundaries to act suggest a national abulia that stifles progress on every level. Significantly, a few people take direct and decisive action. One is Florita's mother, who leads the most elemental existence of any character, to the point of being inarticulate, yet goes to the police to say, "He wasn't the one" again and again, thus saving Pedro. The other is Cartujo, the miserable, self-styled boyfriend of Florita who, quite consistent with his primitive mentality, insists on "an eye for an eye" and kills Dorita.

The separation among the classes is spatial as well as social: the *chabola* slum is removed from the urban center; the middle class seemingly exists on a remote island in the city, and Ortega's lecture sponsored by the upper-class elite significantly takes place in a building whose lower floor houses a servants' dance: "As in any well-ordered cosmos, the one in which the event [Ortega's lecture] was taking place was arranged in superimposed spheres placed one on the other" (130).

The tangential affinity that *Tiempo de silencio* may show with the concerns of the social novel is offset by any number of factors indicating that Martín-Santos is writing in another mode. The strong emphasis on individual concerns is not the least of the differences. The satirical manner of class presentation separates *Tiempo de silencio* from the technique and intent of neorealism: Martín-Santos does not emphasize the representational or collective symbolism of the individual. Natural though it may be to associate the major and secondary characters with their class, each one has such obvious uniqueness that the representational quality is not as apparent. This change is accomplished mainly with self-presentation through interior monologue, which subjectively evaluates the character's present circumstances and allows an admixture of past history, ambitions, and individual impressions.

Pedro's lack of identification with a single class allows his journey through the many levels of society. His own professional, social, and personal aspirations reveal a series of conflicts that enhance the dialectical realism of the work. The individual versus the "system" is a strong thematic constant in *Tiempo,* the system in this case encompassing any group whose narrow self-definition will not permit the flexibility necessary for individual development (rules, codes of behavior, etc.). The urban environment, which envelops and stifles, comes under attack (". . . man cannot get lost even if he wants to because one thousand, ten thousand, one hundred thousand pairs of eyes classify and arrange him, recognize and embrace him, identify and save him" [17]); the rigidity and pompous condescension of the director of the institute, who fires Pedro; the social system, which traps Pedro into marriage; the legal and penal codes, which must "remove" Pedro from society because of his transgressions; and finally, even the primitive vengeance, which causes his ultimate withdrawal—all are elements that force the "time of silence" on Pedro.

As a psychiatrist, Martín-Santos was well versed in the theory of psychological developmental stages through which an individual might pass, and his special interest was existential psychology, a field in which he had published professional studies.[8] Pedro's personal development and self-realization (or lack thereof) may be seen in the light of this branch of psychology, with its emphasis on the necessity of objective separation from one's past, the formation and implementation of a code of conduct or project that would not only reveal but direct a mode of behavior clearly indicating one's beliefs, and the final acceptance of one's life in relationship to others. The recognition of a project suggests life as constant evolution or "becoming." Shifting narrative perspectives in *Tiempo* chronicle the protagonist's self-awareness, the acceptance of his past, and his integration and assumption of responsibility for his acts.[9]

Whether applied specifically to individual development from a psychological point of view or regarded in a wider philosophical framework, existentialism helps to explain the behavior and ultimate fate of Pedro. Many philosophical tenets of existentialism are present in his adventures: the conflict between the self and the other, the individual's struggle for personal freedom, the sudden realization of the absurdity of existence and the resultant anguish, the desire for self-definition and authenticity, the idea of individual guilt, the necessity of choice and responsibility, and final solitude and alienation. Pedro's soliloquy in jail has been signaled as one of the most existential monologues in the contemporary Spanish novel.[10]

A final thematic level—and one that will play a significant part as forerunner to the New Novel—is the national dimension Martín-Santos introduces on real, symbolic, and allegorical levels. In effect, *Tiempo* refers as much to Spain's situation as it does to the individual plight of Pedro. The economic and scientific backwardness of the country is symbolized in Pedro's inability to carry out further research. The benchmark in this case is the United States, with its endless supplies of mice, money, and clean laboratories. The introduction of other nations as points of comparison indicates the author's national concern: the ironical contrasts with the United States, the anthropological comparison with primitive nations, and religious practices of India paired with Hispanic culture are among many parallels drawn from foreign countries to provide examples of the place of Spain within a global perspective. Thus the narrow field of Pedro's research embraces a national allegory with the implication of determinism (essential historical character) versus self-determination (possibility of change). Cancer becomes a metaphor: if it is viral, there is hope for change, since a remedy may be possible with a vaccine; transmitted genetically, there is no hope of cure.

In his criticism of national situations, Martín-Santos transcends his own historical period or, at most, uses the present only as a point of departure to analyze the Spanish character. His concern with "The Problem of Spain" aligns the author with those of the Generation of 1898, the most obvious forerunner being Valle-Inclán, whose *esperpentos* attack the superficial, pompous self-image of Spain. Martín-Santos finds that this image is in direct conflict with the reality proven by history and the Spanish character. *Tiempo* is the first in a series of works seeking to find or expose the roots of the Problem of Spain and forming a bond of common interest in later manifestations of the New Novel. This makes Goya a significant artistic link between Valle-Inclán (whose definition of the *esperpento* gives a prominent place to Goya's techniques of distortion) and *Tiempo*, whose central reference to Goya's famous painting of the Witches' Sabbath leaves no doubt concerning Martín-Santos's leadership in using art as a technique in the demythologizing of "Official Spain." Significantly, this novel was the first of a projected trilogy entitled "La destrucción de la España sagrada" (The destruction of sacred Spain). [11]

Martín-Santos's tendency to use many ostensibly plot-related events to elucidate Spain's situation demonstrates his propensity toward metonymic literary structures. An excellent example of this may be found in the description of cities, a generalization that in fact refers only initially to Madrid and ultimately to Spain's history and present unfortunate condition. [12]

The conflict of instinct versus culture, or the clash of primitivism and decadency (i.e., overcivilization), is caught up in the motif of sexuality, whose primitive aspect appears in the incest of Muecas, its perversion in the prostitutes, its biological limits in the hormonal imbalance and menopause associated with the middle class, and its exploitation not only in prostitution but in the use of sex to trap Pedro into marriage (in which case the former is the more honest of the two). It reveals the mystique of *machismo* (the grandmother's pride in her husband's abuse of her, his insatiable sexual appetites and virility) and informs the honor code filtered down to the lowest class and interpreted in its most violent form.[13] Finally, the application of the sexual metaphor extends to the national situation, in which women worship the virility of the he-goat; but, conversely, the castration of the male is equivalent to the time of silence, a metaphor of powerlessness in which the system, circumstance, or a lack of direction eventually emasculates the individual, taking away his initiative and making him conform: "Pedro listens to the sound of the train wheels and muses 'why am I not in despair? It's comfortable to be a eunuch, it's peaceful to be deprived of testicles, in spite of being castrated, it's pleasant to take the air and the sun while you dry up in silence' " (238).

A highly subjective interpretation of point of view and language complements the ideas in the novel. *Tiempo* manipulates various perspectives, some of which are not clearly identifiable (e.g., the division between Pedro-narrator and Pedro-protagonist; the question as to whom, ultimately, the narrative voice belongs).[14] Interior monologue, conversation, reported speech *(estilo indirecto libre)*, an "impartial" narrative voice, and a blend of various styles and perspectives heighten Pedro's self-development. Martín-Santos offers contrasting interior monologues, each presented in the appropriate style, to form a counterpoint of class and concern with Pedro's voice. Examples may be found in the monologues of the grandmother, of Cartucho, and of Similiano, each of which endows the character with enough individuality to remove him from the representational status associated with the social novel.

Further evidence of authorial presence is readily available in comments, ironical or sarcastic remarks, diatribes, apostrophes, and the liberal use of rhetorical devices that control the narrative point of view. One critic signals Martín-Santos's technique of "equivocation": "The mastery of the novelist is revealed by his capacity to give description for what is, in essence, an interpretation."[15] Manipulation is evident also in the deliberate use of literary convention to mislead the reader, such as high-flown language to convey a vulgar, commonplace event, pseudoobjective, scientific terminology to present particularly emotional issues (the world of the *chabolas*), objective reportage (the unreal system of vertical burials), and emotion-charged language (diatribe to the he-goat in the Goya painting). Such distortions make the reader aware of the real situation in Spain, hidden behind official rhetoric.[16]

Martín-Santos's interest in stretching the commonly accepted limitations imposed on language has raised the medium to a position of unexpected importance. From the simple, straightforward prose of neorealism, he moves to long, complex, and often recondite sentences, distorted by random thoughts or comments. The vocabulary undergoes considerable expansion with the addition of diverse lexical systems: technical (medical, psychiatric, anthropological, sociological), cultural (mythical, literary, philosophical, artistic), business or commercial, and uniquely national (historical or folkloric). Martín-Santos also adds words or phrases from other languages (English, French, Latin), which he sometimes transcribes into the Spanish phonetic system (e.g., *mideluéstico,* an adjective meaning "from the Middle West"). He combines words to invent new ones: Dorita is *"no-madre-no-doncella"* ("neither-mother-nor-maid" [108]). He employs unusual or Latinate constructions to give the impression of literary, high-flown Spanish, alternated with the low-class slang of Cartucho.

The expansion of linguistic and rhetorical possibilities is only one indication of the highly complex nature of *Tiempo de silencio.* The novel is also the first of a literary mode called the neobaroque, a particularly apt term suggesting the intellectual, elitist stance of many writers of the Spanish Golden Age. Martín-Santos has adapted a baroque vision to a contemporary situation, thus creating dual planes that complement his theory on the unchanging nature of Spain. To traditional rhetorical or literary devices (apostrophe, metaphor, ellipsis, periphrasis, and many others) he adds contemporary literary devices such as interior monologue, stream of consciousness, and a multitude of narrative voices. Latinate vocabulary is still more noticeable, in addition to scientific and technical lexicons, foreign words, and contemporary neologisms. To the formal use of antithesis the novelist adds man's constant tension between his intimate and his social role. Whereas the disillusionment associated with the classic baroque vision was framed within a religious context, Martín-Santos presents an ultimately existential vision of the absurdity of existence, and the ironic stance of the baroque writer becomes black humor and the desperation that culminates in the final metaphor of silence and castration.

Stylistically, the baroque influence is pervasive in *Tiempo;* specific references establish the temporal parallels even further. Cervantes and his *Quijote* are raised from intertextual reference to one of the themes of the work. Martín-Santos continuously refers to the man, the book, and the age in which he lived. In a long section structured by the symbolic form of the spiral, the reader receives a contemporary interpretation of the *Quijote:* the more beautiful (but false) world of chivalry that Quijano tried to impose on reality, and the fact that his madness "consists only of believing in the possibility of improving [reality]" (63). Certain biographical parallels link the two novelists: their stay in jail, their reaction to their times, the use of the literary text as national criticism and catharsis, and their disillusionment.

Although the baroque influence is noticeable throughout the novel both in construction and allusion, there are abundant examples of other national and foreign sources that considerably widen the sphere of the work. Sartre, Bergson, Dilthey, and Jaspers offer philosophical sources; Joyce's influence is apparent in the interior monologue, stream of consciousness, and the modernization and application of myth to a contemporary situation. Proust's careful prose and psychological interests are evident, as is Kafka's depiction of man's lack of control and alienation in a universe whose unwritten laws he cannot decipher. Martín-Santos's self-acknowledged interests range from English and German novelists to his various professional readings.

The select audience to which this novel is undisguisedly directed constitutes another distinct divergence from the aims of the social novel, whose intentions of direct action or denunciation implied accessibility to a wider audience, with no aesthetic overlay to cloud the message. While *Tiempo* can be understood on the most obvious plot level, further layers in the form of leitmotifs can best be appreciated by those who can grasp the nature of the references. In addition to the intertextual sections, Martín-Santos uses Freudian psychology and the return to the womb (as in Pedro's stay in jail);

the ever-present descent and return motif is linked to Pedro's journey, which has been studied by several critics in the light of classical mythology (Pedro as Ulysses; the hero myth);[17] and he constantly alludes to myth or legend (Florita as the unfortunate Nausikaa, the middle-class women as the three fates, Cartucho as the cyclops, Pedro's descent into the "underworld" [jail]). *Tiempo de silencio* deserves its place of importance for its complexity, sincerity of vision, and multilevel planes of reality. Later novelists seized and adapted the innovations of *Tiempo de silencio,* but few managed to achieve its unique character, combining tradition and innovation, national, social, and individual perspectives into a complex summa,[18] truly "inimitable and unrepeatable."

Chapter Nine
The New Novel

A movement began to take shape in Spanish novelistic literature in the late 1960s, characterized by discarding the thematic and formal guidelines of neorealism in favor of a totally new interpretation of the functions of literature.[1] The New Novel—the term applied to this manifestation—attempts to transcend neorealism and to subvert our conceptions about material existence. The new themes associated with the movement do not completely ignore national or social issues, but they often subordinate them to questions concerning the very nature and perception of reality itself. Although no precise date separates previous literary styles from the new movement, 1972 is the year by which the change had gained recognition as an entity in its own right. By this time, the socially oriented themes of later neorealism had played themselves out, and their authors not only considered them passé but often disavowed them completely. This date also marks the appearance of several key works of the new group.

As the direction of the New Novel became more easily identifiable, various groups associated with its emergence gained recognition. As with any literary trend, however, there is a good deal of overlapping of characteristics in the younger writers as well as those established novelists who adapted their themes to the New Novel.[2] In the older group are those writers who were never associated with neorealism: Juan Benet, Gonzalo Torrente Ballester, Alvaro Cunqueiro, Antonio Prieto, Carlos Rojas. Some writers had a primary association with neorealism and later changed to the more radically experimental area of the New Novel. In this group are some who were already on the fringes of the New Novel because of their affiliation with subjective neorealism (Matute, Delibes, Juan Goytisolo, Ana María Moix, Juan Marsé, and the ever-experimental Cela), but also those who clearly abandoned their allegiance to the social or objectivist novel: Luis Goytisolo, Alfonso Grosso, Antonio Ferres, Jesús López Pacheco, José Manuel Caballero Bonald, Juan García Hortelano, Jesús Fernández Santos, Ramón Nieto, Jorge

Trulock, and many others. Finally, a younger group of novelists, whose aesthetic principles never were sympathetic with neorealism (or at best had only an early, tenuous connection with it), developed their literary interests in accord with the new trends, among them Luis Alemany, Javier del Amo, Mariano Antolín Rato, Félix de Azúa, Juan Cruz Ruiz, José María Guelbenzu, J. Leyva, August Martínez Torres, Vicente Molina-Foix, Germán Sánchez Espeso, Javier Tomeo, Jesús Torbado, Carlos Trías, José María Vaz de Soto, and Hector Vázquez Azpiri.

A number of factors helped to create a propitious climate for the New Novel. The decline in popularity of social realism in the international marketplace signaled clearly that a change was in order. The relaxation of censorhip restrictions allowed access to a great number of hitherto unattainable works, as well as the latest currents of international fiction. *"Operación retorno"*—the return and subsequent lionization of exiled writers—opened up a whole new branch of literature to Spanish residents through the extensive publication of the exiles' works and the literary prizes associated with their "discovery." Finally, changes in the economic situation affected the cultural scene. The influx of tourism, a brighter economic outlook, increased opportunities for travel or exchange of ideas—information more readily and rapidly accessible through the media gave Spaniards a greater scope for comparison. One theory links changes in the novel at this time with Spain's shift from an underdeveloped country to a consumer-oriented society. Literature parallels this transformation by abandoning the objectivist techniques in an attempt to penetrate surface appearances and investigate a global sense of reality.[3]

An overview of postwar literature will reveal that there had been ample preparation for the appearance of the New Novel.[4] Subjective neorealism antedates the innovational character of the New Novel in subject matter and in some of the formal innovations. Both movements employ interiorization to reveal a unique, hermetic world, temporal experimentation in form and theme, and the incorporation of memoir, myth, paradigm, and the universal dimension.

A small number of writers not allied with the Mid-Century Generation had developed mythic and fantastic literature, but they were relatively unknown because of their divergence from the more popular mode. Alvaro Cunqueiro's fiction has always included elements that transcend phenomenal reality through myth, fantasy, magic, legend, and an air of timelessness, as well as unusual and impressive erudition conveyed with an ornate prose style (all characteristics of the "new" literature). *Un hombre que se parecía a Orestes* (A man who looked like Orestes) won the 1969 Nadal prize, a sure indication of the acceptance of nonrealism in Spanish literature. Rafael Sánchez Ferlosio's *Industrias y andanzas de Alfanhuí* (Labors and wanderings of Alfanhuí, published as *Alfanhuí*, 1951) departed radically from neorealism. A strange, dreamlike atmosphere surrounds the experiences of young Alfanhuí. Language and fantasy complement each other to create a highly lyrical, imaginative novel.

On the fringes of neorealism, the Metaphysical Group (see pp. 76–77 above) is aesthetically on the threshold of the New Novel because of their interest in transcending historical and documentary reality and their intellectual conception of the novel. As the pendulum of literary taste swung to include their unique type of fiction, many writers received long-overdue recognition. Gonzalo Torrente Ballester had written symbolic, experimental, or mythical novels since 1942; in 1972 he received two literary prizes for his *Saga/fuga de J.B.* Carlos Rojas received the 1979 Nadal Prize for *El ingenioso hidalgo y poeta Federico García Lorca asciende a los infiernos* (The ingenious hidalgo and poet Federico García Lorca ascends into hell), but he has long since developed his unusual themes and style in the relationship between artist and creation (*Aquelarre* [Witches' Sabbath, 1970]).

The single most important factor to determine the course of the New Novel within Spain was the introduction and popularity of recent Spanish American literature. The year 1962, in which Mario Vargas Llosa received the Seix Barral prize for *La ciudad y los perros* (The city and the dogs, published as *The Time of the Hero*) marks the inception of the subsequent "Latin American invasion."[5] Publisher Carlos Barral was again instrumental in fomenting new aesthetic tastes, recognizing the importance of the Spanish American "Novel of the Boom" and introducing several such works in his *Nueva Narrativa Hispánica* series. Some Spaniards viewed the extreme popularity of the Americans with a measure of suspicion,[6] but recognized the positive aspects of the Boom in the creation of an atmosphere for experimental works.[7] In 1972 two publishing companies, Planeta and Barral Editores, ushered in the new Spanish literature with great fanfare. Barral's announcement of his series was headed by the words "Does a New Spanish Literature Exist or Doesn't It?," a query answered by a spate of critical opinions. Smaller book companies also promoted the new literature: Akal Editor and Jucar have introduced radically experimental works.

The greatest divergence between the New Novelists and those of the neorealistic school is in the diminished preeminence of historical or environmental reality and of the committed approach to art (i.e., art at the service of a specific aim). In its place, the writers fashion a complex piece that may examine our assumptions about the natural order of the world or the foundations of contemporary life. The undermining of so many givens (such as nature, economy, language, myth, tradition) questions the stability of contemporary reality, signaling one major ideological direction of the New Novel, even though each individual work may select a different approach for its particular expression. With the rejection of the mimetic mode, the specific, historically linked criticisms give way to a more universal interpretation, often with cosmic or metaphysical implications.

The result of this new perspective is a contrived ambiguity that permeates the New Novel in every aspect, contradicting much of what the reader has come to expect as literary tradition. Replacing the conventions of logical causality of plot or identifiably developing characters are a number of central ideas around which the work incessantly revolves: mysterious or unidentified protagonists, inversions and fragmentations thematically played against one another much in the manner of a musical fugue, and the coexistence of a strange, mysterious dimension within the natural order. The advent of the novel-puzzle (a variation on the detective novel), in which the novelist provides fragments of the total picture piecemeal in no specific order, involves the reader heavily in the co-creation of the text. Enigma on all fictional levels is a constant in these works.[8]

The shift from the straightforward presentation of facts and scenes to a complex mode of narration is the stylistic complement of the ideas presented above. The reader may perceive reality only from a single, narrow, and interior point of view, which distorts it to the point of unrecognizability, or, conversely, from a distant, superior plane (a psychological distortion in the first case; a cosmic vision in the second). The plot or informing idea is more intellectually conceived, or so interiorized as to be alogical. The cathartic element of the psychoanalytic process is evident in several works, at times applied on the national level (Goytisolo's *Señas de identidad* [*Marks of Identity*, 1966] or *Reivindicación del conde don Julián* [The claim of Count Julian, published as *Count Julian*, 1970).

Conventions of external and internal representation are no longer valid, giving the impression of disembodied voices rather than flesh-and-blood people. It is common to confuse protagonists or to discover doubles presented through various techniques (such as fragmentation or a mirroring effect). Any number of works develop this theme: Félix de Azúa's *Las lecciones de Jena;* J. Leyva's *La circumcisión del señor Solo* (The circumcision of Mr. Solo, 1972), Vicente Molina-Foix's *Museo provincial de los horrores* (Provincial museum of horrors, 1970). The author may employ metamorphosis (Delibes's *Parábola del náufrago* [Parable of a drowning man, 1969]); equivocation, or doubling, may occur on a temporal plane (*Saga/fuga,* in which the hero transmigrates in time through a series of other J.B.s). The disregard for physical appearance is complemented by the lack of names (Martínez Torres's *Fases de la luna* [Phases of the moon], 1974) or by the modification or confusion of names within the text (*Volverás a Región* [You will return to Region, 1967], by Juan Benet, uses several versions of the same name to apply to a single character) or multiple names (a character in López Pacheco's *La hoja de parra* [The fig leaf, 1973] refers to himself as "Peter II the Good, presently Peter II the Notary . . . , Pedro I in Cruelty and Atheism"[9]).

To the modification of traditional character development the writers add a deliberately elusive plot. Although a specific idea or theme may inform the novel, this idea may not be immediately apparent from an ordinary reading of the text. In place of story—or as accompaniment to the plot—the reader discovers a series of associated thematic clusters that recur in ever-changing fashion and, if considered in their totality, offer a complex and multilevel picture of reality. Such nonsequential action also comments on human perception of reality, which is simultaneous rather than linear. The narration of a single event may be viewed from various angles (Benet's *Volverás* or Juan Marsé's *Si te dicen que caí* [The Fallen, 1973]). Extreme examples are the experimental novels of Guelbenzu: *Antifaz* (Veil, 1970) offers several versions of a single occurrence (David's suicide), all negated or questioned when he appears in the last scene of the novel.

An unspecified locale reinforces the ambiguity of character and situation. It may be possible to glimpse or intuit identifiable places (León in Benet, Andalusia in Caballero Bonald's *Agata, ojo de gato* (Cat's eye agate, 1974), but the tenuous connections create a hermetic yet credible society with internal laws. The setting in *Agata,*

for example, falls within a time frame that "no longer possessed a
. . . correspondence of any kind with the daily transaction of history."[10] The incorporation of supernatural or mysterious elements
likewise characterizes some new novels. Alvaro Cunqueiro, Torrente
Ballester, Benet, and Carlos Rojas, to a greater or lesser degree,
have constantly introduced these elements into their works. Their
presence generally seems to symbolize the complexity of existence,
which consists of more than apprehensible phenomena.

The New Novel fragments unity and fashions a nightmarish scenery devoid of traditional environmental associations. A notable disregard for exterior reality (e.g., rooms filled with furniture,
descriptions of nature, or even of other people) displaces the landscape inward, creating the impression that modern theories of determinism have given way to something both unique and mysterious.
This technique partially explains the vacuum that seemingly surrounds the characters: the absence of traditional social contacts and
the lack of identification with the everyday world have removed the
last vestige of external logic.

One environmental element of interest remains in the New Novel:
the presence of mysterious, often threatening natural forces. The
characters, only too cognizant of this presence, take pains to avoid
or mollify them. The malevolent guard Numa personifies Región's
menacing infraworld; a hedge closes inward to choke out Jacinto's
rebellion in *Parábola del náufrago;* the intrusive, seething swamp is
an ever-present factor in *Agata, ojo de gato.* These elements suggest
irrational and uncontrollable powers of uncertain origin, symbolizing man's inability to control his universe by reason, learning, or
technology. The primitive, dark side of life prevails, implying a
cyclical return to prehistory, where one cannot apply laws of logic
and where man's gods are unfathomable natural forces.

The creation of a cosmic vision is the natural consequence of these
generalities, since the internal logic of the piece allows for the
construction of a world containing its own apparatus and premises.
The protagonists are no longer bound by the same laws as the readers,
and so accept the system, however bizarre, as part of the natural
order. The system may be totally oppressive, as in *Parábola del
náufrago,* with its bureaucratic hierarchies and its "God" as the head
of the company; it may be mythical, as in *Sagalfuga*'s city of Castroforte, which levitates and is not located on any map; its minimal
connection with the rest of Spain (Benet's Región) may allow for

the intrusion of rites and myth in uneasy coexistence with tanks and armies; or it may display a suggestively medieval setting (Ana María Matute's *La torre vigía* [The watch tower], 1969) or primeval implications *(Agata, ojo de gato)*.

The shift in geographical and historical specificity allows a wider interpretive scope. Such abstractions suggest the expansion of the idea to a metonymic or allegorical level (the region then being the abstract version of the specific locale), a fact borne out even in titles such as *Parábola* and *Sagalfuga*. Ramón Nieto's *La señorita* (The lady, 1974) offers an explanatory page preceding the text to indicate the symbolic and interchangeable nature of the vague setting.[11] The reader learns that

The indications
NORTH

WEST   EAST

SOUTH
could be substituted for
UP

LEFT   RIGHT

DOWN
or also for
PALACE

CHALET   GYMNASIUM

TOWN

These symbols can be understood most clearly on a historical level, as one critic has noted in an article discussing political allegory in the contemporary Spanish novel;[12] however, allegory is present in other forms, particularly in existential subjects.

Despite the universality created by these new locales and unusual plots, most novelists have traces of criticism associated with Spain's conditions. While varying in interpretations as to specifics, most readers can infer connections with (and therefore commentaries on) Spain: the Civil War raging in Región; the strange setting in *Agata, ojo de gato,* which, in the words of one critic, offers an explanation of Spain's contemporary problems;[13] in *Parábola,* an archetypal repressive society evokes thoughts of Franco and his political system through the portrayal of the leader don Abdón,[14] while the strange political allegory of Jesús Torbado's *La construcción del odio* (The construction of hatred, 1969) suggests Franco and the Valley of the Fallen to one reviewer.[15]

Variations on eschatology thread their way through much of this literature. In addition to the constant references to death or withdrawal on a personal level, one perceives a more pervasive sense of finality. On one hand, decadence and ruin appear constantly; on the other, aggressive violence and apocalyptic destruction metaphorically raze the foundations of culture. Examples of the first are apparent in all of Benet's Región novels, in Matute's *La torre vigía,* and in Luis Goytisolo's *Recuento,* which ends with images of contemporary and ancient (Pompeii, Machu Picchu) ruins associated with destructive time, and in chronicles of family decadence or extinction (*Agata, ojo de gato,* Alfonso Grosso's *Florido mayo* [Flowered May, 1973], or Vázquez Azpiri's *Corrido de Vale Otero,* 1974). Juan Goytisolo's *Reivindicación del conde don Julián* and *Juan sin tierra* typify destructive aspects of the New Novel, openly parodying the foundations of the culture that has betrayed the protagonist. Following in Goytisolo's footsteps are those bitter, parodic memoirs slashing at the culture responsible for the formation of the protagonists (*Hoja de parra,* and to some extent Vaz de Soto's *El infierno y la brisa* [Hell and the breeze, 1971], concerning childhood education in a religious setting), although these are not destructive fantasies in the same way.

Although criticism of Spain may be present explicitly or implicitly, these works are not social novels because they do not describe the historical situation so much as the conditioning or larger system of cultural values that create character. Many novels treat individual introspection: a maladjusted or alienated individual takes stock of his personal, national, or cultural past in a desperate attempt to understand himself. The antihero searches for the roots of his estrangement, a parodic or inverted quest revealing false gods and a destructive, ironic stance. This bitter attitude complements the novels that create new myths based on the destruction of old ones. Once the cathartic process of analysis is complete, there may be hope for new values.

The use of myth and introspection includes a reevaluation of the place of time, a topic of interest to the subjective neorealists as well. The coexistence of the past within the present is the subject of many novels of retrospection, bolstered with dizzying fragmentation and temporal as well as episodic rearrangements (among others, Antonio Ferres's *Ocho, siete, seis* [Eight, seven, six, 1972] and Grosso's *Florido mayo*) as well as such usual techniques as synchronic and psychological time.

The mysterious coexistence of time frames expands our conception of reality as the ghosts of the past determine the lives of the characters (sometimes within a historical framework, as in Benet's *La otra casa de Mazón* [Mazón's other house, 1973], sometimes in a psychological sense) or time periods may merge (Martínez Torres's *Fases de la luna,* 1974) or burst into fragments (the dislocation into past, present, and future paralleling various aspects of the personality in Leyva's *La circumcisión del señor Solo*), while the cyclic nature of life appears in the reiteration motif, as well as through repetitive characters— in time, as in *Sagalfuga de J.B.*, or in character ambiguity through merging or doubling. Time may become the object of intellectual disquisitions, as character or author discusses the effects of time, myth, or memory and its unreliable nature (Benet, for example).

Similarly ambiguous are the works about novelists writing novels (among them, Guelbenzu's *El mercurio,* in which the novelist writes a novel called *El mercurio* (and in which Guelbenzu himself appears as a character), Luis Goytisolo's *Recuento* and the second part of his projected tetralogy, *Los verdes del mayo hasta la mar* [The green of May unto the sea, 1976], or, to a certain degree, the narrations within the narration of *Sagalfuga de J.B.*). The visual image of depth and the continuous movement inward associated with the Chinese box suggest a latent reality just beyond one's grasp.

The labyrinth, which contains both classical and contemporary implications, appears regularly accompanied by mystery, puzzlement, symbolic night journeys, potential self-discovery, or epiphany. The intricate features of Benet's works contain this image on both physical and interior levels; the Casa del Barco *(Sagalfuga)* is an architectural maze;[16] Juan Goytisolo's iconoclastic tour of the vagina of Isabel the Catholic is the parodic rendition of the metaphor. The visual images of the motifs (depth and continuous movement inward in the case of the Chinese box; intricacy and bewilderment associated with the labyrinth) emphasize the philosophy that empirical reality is only a false reflection of a deeper side of life and that a more profound reality may lie beyond one's apperceptions.

Many new novelists are intellectuals who incorporate highly speculative theories of philosophy, mythology, or metaphysics into their works. The "plot" may be the elaboration of certain abstractions much in the manner of an essay, in which story and character are subordinated to the idea. Another subject of unusually heavy interest is metafiction: works about literature that investigate the nature of fiction or language, the relationship of language and art to life, to literature, or to the fabrication of a transcendent reality, or the symbiotic dependence of creator and creation. In Luis Goytisolo's *Recuento,* Raúl decides to create a new type of novel, considerably more inclusive than flat realism and even self-generating (625), and thus affirms his existence through creation; Carlos Rojas's *Aquelarre* blurs the boundaries between reality and art as the subjects from well-known paintings come to life and interact with the characters. Ana María Moix's *Walter ¿por qué te fuiste?,* which shares some of the characteristics of the New Novel, begins and ends with the creation of the very text that the author is living. José María Guelbenzu's *El mercurio* deals with literature on both theoretical and existential levels: there are long discussions about writing with one of the characters, who is also writing a novel called *El mercurio.* In certain novels, metafiction is raised to metacriticism, by composing a literary work within the text, then commenting on it as if it were real (as with José Bastida's explication of his own poetry in *Saga/fuga*).

The reasons for selecting metafictional subjects vary according to the authors: literary criticism (Guelbenzu or Goytisolo, who criticize social realism), philosophical or metaphysical commentary (Rojas's *Aquelarre*), or parody (*Saga/fuga; Reivindicación*). An additional theme is the creative power of the word: the artist creates and is created by language, which can ultimately shape reality. Not surprisingly, several of these novels about writing are actually quests or investigations on an existential as well as a literary level.

Intertextual literary references add a second metafictional level by inserting literature within literature. The piece that the characters discuss, read, or quote, or that the author may cite as a means of indirect commentary, binds the reader closely to the text through a common literary experience. Works from all ages or countries appear in this context: the constant literary allusions and epigraphs in *El mercurio*, the parallels to Du Maurier's *Rebecca* in the opening lines of Ana María Moix's *Walter ¿por qué te fuiste?*, the quotations and analyses from a literary anthology (Vaz de Soto's *Diálogos del anochecer* [Dialogues at nightfall, 1971]) are only a few examples. Goytisolo's destructive use of literature is apparent in his bitterly parodic reworking of the Spanish classics in *Reivindicación*.

The metafictional discussion of the nature and function of literature reveals a new nonfictional phenomenon: the critic-creator. Juan Benet's theoretical works analyze the creative act (among several, *La inspiración y el estilo* [Inspiration and style, 1966]); Goytisolo continually analyzes the new directions and possibilities for literature (as in *El furgón de cola* [Caboose, 1967]); while Torrente Ballester, Félix Grande, and others are also literary critics.

The elevation of language to an end in itself is one of the distinguishing features of the New Novel. Such interest fits into the intellectual and revisionist nature of this literature and its methods of distancing between text and author through the analytic mode. Recondite words, neologisms, Latinate structures, foreign vocabulary, scientific or technical terms, and rhetorical devices reinforce the intellectual cast. Juxtaposed with this are the popular manifestations of speech: street slang, abundant scatologic or pornographic terms, swearing, contemporary slogans, phrases from advertising, lines from popular songs and movies, which in turn raise popular culture to a literary level. Other types of communication include fragments of political speeches, newspaper articles, police reports, media accounts, as well as consciously high-flown literary language. Examples abound: Goytisolo's trilogy becomes increasingly dependent on linguistic collage; Guelbenzu's *El mercurio* contains an admixture of different speech patterns. Fragmentation, collage, and linguistic polyphony are also apparent in works by Grosso, Leyva, Vázquez Azpiri, and many others.

Many writers look at language as the perpetuator of certain cultural systems and values through meanings so deeply ingrained that their powerful effect is lost through habit. In the criticism of contemporary reality, it is natural to turn to communication as the very foundation of cultural tradition, and to mock official rhetoric, pat phrases, social or political catch-words, etc., to reveal a static, dehumanized society. This is particularly effective in alternation with a highly personal and introspective form of expression, as in Goytisolo's *Reivindicación* or *Juan sin tierra*.

Forcing both syntax and grammatical structure beyond conventional usage, the writers attempt to question reality by subverting its modes of expression. In fact, the criticism of reality may be just as strong as that in the social novel, but the manner of attack differs substantially. Some novels eschew conventional forms of punctuation, employ run-on sentences that continue for pages (Benet's *Meditación* [Meditation, 1970], *Fases de la luna*), omission of capital letters (in Cela's *Oficio de tinieblas* [Tenebrae office, 1973]), or, in *Parábola del náufrago* (for specific purposes), show a disregard for any punctuation *(El mercurio, Antifaz)*, or use thought clusters rather than complete grammatical units *(Reivindicación)*. Such techniques reinforce the awareness of language at a cognitive level, suggesting its modification from functional entity to autonomous subject. Language and syntax that are so highly complex stand apart from their more neutral functions as conveyers of ideas. This technique is particularly apparent in the case of those novels that treat writing and the creative act as the subject: Luis Goytisolo's complex sentences in *Recuento;* Guelbenzu's *El mercurio.*

As if in defiance of fixed communication patterns, several protagonists invent their own language: Jacinto in *Parábola del náufrago* creates his own tongue, as does the protagonist in *Sagalfuga.* Although there is some precedent for this (Pérez de Ayala's character is *Belarmino y Apolonio* [1921] also fashioned his own hermetic language; Alfanhuí had to leave school because he had learned a strange alphabet that no one could understand), the invention of new linguistic systems suggests adanic implications that complement the mythic cosmovision in other novels. The necessity to re-create the world takes form in reinventing the word. José Bastida's explanation for devising a personal language to express the depths of complex reality parallels the aims of the New Novel: he wants to transmit "what things are and are not at the same time, the visible and invisible facets, the outside and the inside . . ." (508).

The invention of a new language may be symbolic of a higher reality; the destruction of language may conversely signify the apocalyptic razing of civilization. The clearest proponent of this is Juan Goytisolo, who as early as 1967 had criticized the static quality of language with an artistic call to arms: "The world in which we live demands a new, virulent and anarchic language. In the vast and overloaded warehouse of antiques that is our language, we can only create by destroying: a destruction that is simultaneously creation, a creation that is at the same time destructive."[17] Much of what he says here is put into practice in *Reivindicación del conde don Julián,* but the most extreme application of his theory appears in *Juan sin tierra (Juan the Landless),* which ends in verbal chaos.

Language may also be a phenomenon divorced from the extra-textual world. The word, in this case, creates its own reality. *Juan sin tierra* and *Recuento* offer examples of this interest, the latter positing a kind of existential salvation through literary creation. It ends as the alienated Raúl sits down to pen his novel, and the act of writing allows him a breadth of understanding hitherto unknown (623).[18]

The stylistic expansion of narrative voices underlines the fragmentation of reality characteristic of the New Novel. In addition to the traditional third person, the novelists experiment with different means of communication to the reader: the widespread use of the *tú* form (which may suggest, among other ideas, the split between the objective and subjective self);[19] the first-person singular, often a point of departure for the double, and particularly effective in novels of retrospection; the use of polyphony in the mixture of several narrative voices that are at times not clearly defined (see Juan Marsé's *Si te dicen que caí* or López Pacheco's *La hoja de parra*); and the incorporation of intertextuality of all kinds.

The intellectual character and experimental tendencies of the New Novel remove it substantially from the plot-oriented, closed-ended works of neorealism. In its place appears a hybrid form that strains the popular conception of the novel: in addition to minimal plot movement, the authors create a sort of essay novel, apparent not only in the theoretical discussions on any number of subjects (by the characters and even by the author) but in formal modifications as well. This term has been applied to Luis Goytisolo's works,[20] and Cela's *Oficio de tinieblas* bears the following epigraph: "Naturally, this is not a novel but the purging of my heart."[21] In line with the nontraditional format, Cela divides the work into numbered "monads" (perhaps suggesting their autonomy and indivisible nature) ranging in length from one to several pages and covering an enormous range of subjects. Benet effectively experiments with a combination of novel and drama in *La otra casa de Mazón.* The addition of apparatus generally associated with scholarly works adds still another dimension to these novels: footnotes *(Volverás a Región)* and glosses (Benet's *Un viaje de invierno* [A winter's journey, 1972]) deliberately confuse the reader as to the role of the author and the separation between fiction and reality. Further evidence of the desire to destroy conventions is disregard for traditional novelistic divisions: Cela's monads; Vázquez Azpiri's *Fauna* numbers the chapters 6, 6 bis, 7, 7 bis, and so on (10 bis is a blank page on which is printed the letter O), suggesting simultaneity through repetition.

Typographical and spatial innovations signal new trends in visual communication. Some examples selected from numerous instances are double columns *(Fauna)*, unusual word arrangements to give the impression of free verse or concrete poetry *(Reivindicación)*, two superimposed stories separated only by different type (Carlos Rojas's *Auto de fe*, 1968), drawings of different positions of the feet to accompany the subject of walking *(El mercurio)*, lines of a single word, and lines of unusual length.

The renewed interest in music suggests exploration of nonverbal communication (hence the use of musical techniques such as leitmotif and theme with variations). Several novelists indicate their interest by employing musical terms in their works: Benet's *Un viaje de invierno*—the title of a Schubert song-cycle; Torrente Ballester's *Saga/fuga*, which is a play on words, since *fuga* also means "flight"; the title *Leitmotif*, suggesting musical techniques in J. Leyva's novel.[22] Such experimentation with form and terms has in turn prompted critics to coin other words to describe the New Novel, such as antiliterature[23] or "literary creation."[24]

The new interpretations of reality, the complex aesthetic shell that contains them, and the unusual role of the reader in the creative process raise the act of reading to an intellectual exercise. The application of the term neobaroque to the New Novel is thus appropriate to describe the modernized version of *culteranismo* (the intentional obscurity of style) and *conceptismo* (clever or unusual ideas, intellectually conceived works) as well as a philosophy that gives preeminence to aesthetics as expression of a worldview.[25] Questions concerning the ultimate nature of reality and a critical view of life culminating in disillusionment and cynicism (conveyed by various technical means) also link the two literatures. A Hispanic writer expressed the contemporary meaning of the term baroque in today's literature: "Baroque implies attacking, in a very subtle way, the fundamental bases of our civilization. To be baroque is to squander, to waste, to parody materials."[26]

In addition to the influence that Hispanic literature (particularly the Spanish American New Novel) and the various scientific disciplines have exercised on the New Novel, international sources may also have affected its conception and particularly its experimental character. James Joyce and William Faulkner are obvious examples; Kafka and Brecht offer affinities as well. Other English and American writers have left their mark. William Burroughs exercises considerable fascination, as do others of the "Beat Generation," whose destructive literature and depiction of subcultures or popular culture (particularly at their point of intersection with the "establishment") suggest themes of interest to several of the younger writers of the group.

Spanish writers are also familiar with the theories and polemics surrounding the French New Novel. Goytisolo and Castellet had already posed questions concerning literary conventions; the subsequent reaction against traditional literary methods certainly follows their line of reasoning, if not the practical suggestions. However, a second group of French novelists may also have left some theoretical traces on the New Novel: the Nouveau nouveau roman (the New New Novel). Associated at first with the literary journal *Tel Quel,* this group moves from the human angle to the literary process, a theme more and more apparent in the Spanish novels. Like the Spanish writers, several French novelists are also critics: Jean Pierre Faye, Jean Ricardou, Philippe Sollers, and Jean Thibaudeau. Then, too, note should be taken of the technical studies on language and meaning. In addition to the ubiquitous de Saussure and the Russian formalists, other names such as Roman Jakobson and Emile Benveniste appear associated not only with critics but with the novelists themselves.[27]

Considering the changes in the contemporary novel from a historical point of view, one critic has noted a number of characteristics that seem to reflect the end of the Franco era: the tendency toward autobiography or memoir novels, not only as a return to a personal past, but a historical résumé of an entire period—the dictatorship—which was obviously drawing to a close. Such retrospection allows the writer the necessary distance to comprehend the events of the period. The interest in metafiction (creation within creation) is explained as a parallel to the ethical indemnification demanded after the dictatorship. Finally, fantasy is the destruction of the barriers that had constrained the novelists' scope to more immediate problems. The preference for dialogue lays bare "the eternal tension between individuals and society, between the desire for vital communication and personal truth, and the inveterate obligations imposed by the world of laws, between what could have been in an atmosphere of liberty and what surely will not be possible after too many years of oppression."[28] Such a symbolic interpretation of the New Novel's elements shows the insistence with which critics and readers seek to understand themes and forms within the context of the historical framework that produced them.

Although not all critics unqualifiedly approved of the experimental modes introduced with the New Novel,[29] most appreciated the fresh outlook and change of direction that it represented. A combination of literary evolution (the end of one cycle of literature and a consequent search for new directions) and historical circumstances (the change in political policies) fostered the development of this particular form of fiction, whose experimental and universal nature gained acceptance beyond Spanish borders and is even now giving Spanish literature the opportunity to take its place with the international fictional currents of the twentieth century.[30]

Volverás a Región

The years 1972–73 are most often associated with the change from neorealism, but a single work, published five years earlier, signals the first introduction of the New Novel in Spain. *Volverás a Región* (You will return to Región, 1967)[31] was the first extensive fictional work written by Juan Benet, an engineer by profession. The complexity of form and content, and the experimental nature of the narrative, evoked some puzzlement and adverse criticism.[32] Benet's complex and carefully thought out novel moves away from any apparent linear plot. In the words of one Spanish critic, "the plot of the work is practically impossible to disentangle, each new reading belies the provisional hypothesis formulated previously and the author seems to take pleasure in invalidating and confusing his own tracks time and again to the point of reducing the text to a free combinatorial game of a few given elements."[33] *Volverás* vacillates among intersecting temporal planes (prehistory, pre–Civil War, Civil War, narrative present) and interweaves multiple, though often undeveloped, narrative threads. Ambiguity, confusion, mystery, and multiple perspectives are elements that combine with an intricate style to remove the work almost completely from the sphere of realism. Fragments of thought, unexplained events, and references to unknown characters appear, are dropped, and then recur, much in the manner of musical leitmotifs,[34] forcing the reader to relinquish his traditional role and be swept along on a current of imprecise remembrances.

Región is an isolated place that has sunk into spiritual and physical ruin after the Civil War: it is almost deserted, and hostile nature seems to encroach more and more on the ever-present ruins. The minimal plot concerns the return of Marré, who visits Dr. Sebastián's dilapidated sanatorium, where he is keeping a young mental patient. There they speak of their past, alternately evoking their former experiences and memories, each more concerned with his own life and memories than any real interaction. Confused remembrances of Región and surroundings, their childhood, the Civil War, and members of their families mingle, returning obsessively to several focal points, with far-reaching implications. The first one concerns a gambler, whose magical talisman (a gold coin given to him by a mysterious woman) brings him the luck that wins away Gamallo's money and finally his fiancée, María Timoner, with whom the gambler escapes after pinning Gamallo's hand to the table with a knife. The second focus, with the Civil War as frame, involves experiences of Marré and of her father, Gamallo, an officer with the Nationalist forces in pursuit of the Republicans. Finally, Sebastián's frustrated life is the third major topic of the Región puzzle: his silent love of María Timoner, a subsequent marriage he deliberately refuses to consummate, and his death at the hands of the young patient. As the dialogue continues, Marré reveals her opposition to the suppression of natural instincts. Sebastián appears to represent the opposing view, defending tradition and family. Both are killed at the end of the work, leaving silence and ruin as the dominant note. The separate stories are mysteriously interrelated, and, in classical concept, a single event of seemingly little importance eventually brings ruin on an entire family.

The connection between *Volverás* and the realistic novel is visible in the dialectic represented by Marré and Sebastián. The conflict between order and chaos, reason and instinct, nature and culture may ultimately filter down to the conflict between society and the individual, the latter being represented by Marré. Her conflict between sensuality (life, symbolized by sex) and the strict moral code to which she has been educated to conform ends in death at the hands of a mysterious and symbolic figure representing the status quo.

An extensive use of nature contributes strongly to the impression of a cosmic vision that raises all discussion from an individual to a philosophical, even metaphysical, plane. The inhabitants of the area are not in harmony with nature, which dwarfs human events. The opening situation in the novel—an allusion to a hapless traveler, trapped and doomed in the labyrinthine topography of Región— continues with a detailed description of the hostile countryside and finishes the overview with a symbolic "NO TRESPASSING" sign posted at the border of Mantua, a place jealously guarded by a mysterious person called Numa, who reinforces the uneasy alliance between nature and civilization. Numa becomes a larger-than-life figure whose mythological function as a guardian and avenger of higher powers becomes clear. The novel is punctuated with the sounds of his shots and ends with the implication that he kills Marré, the only one to question the established order.

The extensive technical and geographical descriptions reinforce the suggestions of a certain historical immobility, particularly in the sections on geological layering (38 ff.). Both inanimate and animate nature parallel the lack of movement or change in man, demonstrated in the novel through the repetition of human events. Thus a certain type of determinism envelops the inhabitants of this area and is reinforced by the repetition of the same type of behavior in different time periods, intensified stylistically by recurrent themes that, since they are never presented in causal order or always linked with a specific time period, give the impression of cyclic function even when none exists.

Time also reinforces Benet's theory of the instability of reality: past failures are converted by time into "greatness and honor" (14); time can turn upon itself and, inverted, may change: "The present already happened and all that is left to us was what did not happen one day; nor is the past what it was, but rather what it was not; only the future, what is left to us, is what already has been" (245). Further complicating the issue is the presence of memory, which can transpose the heavy weight of time and react with time to alter seemingly immutable reality: "Memory . . . is almost always the vengeance of what did not take place" (115). Marré's return upsets chronological time, causing reality to "decompose in a thousand fragments of a chaotic and gaseous time" (114), and memory "produces a fissure in the apparent cortex of time, through which one sees that memory does not preserve what happened, that the will is ignorant of what will come, that only desire knows how to join them, but . . . it vanishes as soon as the hateful order of time is restored in one's soul" (114). Much of Benet's interpretation of time must be considered through his philosophy of reality, which is an individually perceived phenomenon, never stable, always changing. Neither time nor behavior seems subject to any causal principles. Ruin (with a capital letter) is a power equal to that of nature's destructive force. Ruin is the inevitable result of time and destruction, and its symptoms are expressed in human apathy, numerous signs of decay (dust, humidity, abandonment), and finally in Numa's gunshots, which protect the region from change.

Since a good portion of the novel treats the perception of reality and the unreliable nature of seemingly objective evidence, the author emphasizes shifting dimensions of time as a subtheme. Memory intervenes to alter the indivisible components of time, and a Bergonsian elasticity makes objective time less important than the individual interpretation of it.[35]

Mystery and the supernatural form part of the complex reality that man is unable to fathom, contributing greatly to the nonrealistic aspects of the work. The characters repeatedly allude to mysterious objects or people, such as a telegraph wheel that predicts the future and transmits messages from beyond the grave (123 ff.), the magical properties of the gambler's gold coin, phantom armies, or strange occurrences in the Mantuan region. The most obvious element is the overpowering, menacing presence of a quasi-supernatural being called Numa, who never appears but constantly occupies people's thoughts. Supernatural elements are integrated into the natural order of life through the dispassionate manner in which the characters present them.

The air of uncertainty or mystery extends from plot to narrative technique. The fragmentation and inversion of story line, the partial treatment of themes, and the use of leitmotif in slightly varying form involve the reader in the very questions plaguing the characters; the stable nature of reality can no longer be counted on. Facts change; characters' names are altered (for example, Rumbal, Rembal, Rembla, Rubal, Rumbas, and so on, pp. 29–33). There are even contradictions—a character will modify his story or the narrator may contradict or question a fact. For example, Marré opens her wallet and extracts "a card—an old, yellowed and wrinkled card, with the edges eaten away and dirty (or was it perhaps a photograph?) which she held out to the Doctor" (101).

Characters themselves are not clearly delineated and merge one into the other, either through the same physical characteristics, similar functions, or ambiguity of reference (as with the identification of the boy who eventually kills Doctor Sebastián or the various origins attributed to Numa). Characters often emerge solely from a partial point of view (often their own), providing a one-dimensional, interior perspective that is highly unreliable. The avoidance of physical description or normal actions makes them more like disembodied voices recalling events or people long dead. Thus Benet establishes a sense of mood in contraposition to the traditional action and development of the novel, and that mood is carefully elaborated in detail, with long, complex sentences creating or recalling sensations that the new events or objects in the novel only serve to objectify (e.g., Dr. Sebastián's wife's book on sexual hygiene and her endless needlework objectify her frustration). The symbolic object or action soon displaces the subject in a type of objective correlative that serves as a metonymic device.

One of the overriding themes of *Volverás* is the dialectic established between order (man's control of his life, and by implication of the universe through reason, logic, science, technical implementation) and the primitive chaos (superstition, instinct, nature), which makes man a victim. An aura of fatality or determinism pervades *Volverás* and complements this theme, as is borne out not only in the characters' words and in the plot but also in cyclic time, recurring images associated with certain events (embroidery, the knights fighting) and even in the grammatical structure (the prophetic syntax of "You will return to Región"). The apathy of most of the characters, who passively accept their role—even to the final ruin of the place— is simply another facet of this: "A town that for thirty years had wanted only to lack desires and to let the few it preserved be consumed, which, as the best solution to the uncertainties of the future and the sentence of an unequivocal destiny, had chosen disdain of the present and forgetting the past . . ." (34). The telegraph wheel predicts a violent death for Dr. Sebastián; this prophecy induces him to retire to Región "to await the fulfillment of my destiny—which I neither oppose nor evade" (126).

Many allusions to pagan practices to pacify the gods reinforce the primitive overlay, implying generally a negative, regressive attitude: "It was not a vengeance, but the renewal of the Kronic cycle, the saturnalian festival of an archaic mind that demanded the *regressus ad uterum*, to erase the errors and confusion of the present age and prepare the birth of a new race" (144). Similarly, intricate structural devices complement the narrative ambiguity of polyphony or unidentified narrative sources. The third-person narrative function is further subdivided into footnotes that add information or contradict one of the characters. A footnote to a question posed by the Doctor begins, "The doctor knew very well what she was referring to . . ." (274). Each section contains interpolations in the form of commentaries, remembrances, interjections, asides, subthemes. Long sentences, which sometimes run for pages, can contain any number of loosely connected ideas, often appearing as interruptions or parenthetical commentaries that belie the conversational environment with which the story is framed. Parenthetical remarks provide another perspective while simultaneously breaking the narrative flow. Ellipsis, synechdoche, and grammatical ambiguity (pronouns with no referents) perfectly complement the ambiguity of narrative voices; the contrast between precise technical vocabulary and the subjective tone of the memories laid out by the conversants underlines the polarity of logic and instinct.

Even within the discourse, Benet employs other devices to undermine the conventions of a logical, orderly world. The pseudo-dialogue is punctuated with many rhetorical questions whose unanswered state casts further uncertainty over the entire novel, much in the manner of an unfulfilled quest. Adverbs of doubt abound, and the use of the future or conditional of probability, often employed to forecast events that have actually passed, blurs the time frame. Thus contradictory facts structured with grammatical ambiguity cast doubt on the veracity of the narration or the reliability of the narrator.[36]

The participation of the reader in such a novel increases substantially from his role as interpreter in the objectivist works. The reader must make a concerted effort to understand a novel like *Volverás* because he is responsible for the creation of order out of the chaotic universe contained in the pages. It is no surprise that critics have offered differing interpretations of the scope of the novel, and even of specific events, proof of the open nature of the novel and the ambiguity that leads to greater reader participation.[37]

It would be difficult to point to Spanish antecedents to *Volverás,* particularly in light of the early appearance of the novel. However, Benet's broad cultural, philosophical, and literary knowledge and his theoretical works on literature reveal an unusual intellectual formation that provides clues. Faulkner is one of his favorite writers,[38] and it is possible to see parallels between the hermetic Yoknapatawpha and Región. Hardy and Lowry are also mentioned,[39] and Benet has acknowledged Proust as a favorite author,[40] as well as his admiration for the recent Spanish American novel—Rulfo, Carpentier, Vargas Llosa, and García Márquez share a kinship of ideas, both in theme and in structural experimentation.[41]

Benet's literary vision falls within the scope of neobaroque literature, particularly in his idea of art as an intellectual exercise. Both *conceptismo* and *culteranismo* are readily apparent in *Volverás a Región* as well as in his later works: the first, in his theories of science and time applied to literature; the second, in his particularly complex manner of narration. Finally, baroque pessimism is evident in the themes of decadence, ruin, and decay.

Volverás a Región is the prototype of the New Novel in Spain, containing and developing early on the most characteristic elements of the experimental mode: an intellectual conception of literature, a questioning attitude toward apparently rational, stable reality, the use of myth, the fantastic, and the supernatural to undermine reality, the introduction of an expanded and original lexicon and complex, difficult style, the creation of a coherent and often hermetic universe, introspection or interiorization indicating a lack of concern for present social conditions in favor of a more universal or personal interpretation of life, the combination of memory and time with history in experimental ways, the inclusion of the reader in his relationship with the work in a new way, either as active participant, co-author, or re-creator through such techniques as narrative unreliability, ambiguity, or enigma.

Volverás a Región was not his only novelistic experiment. Benet had clearly discovered a mode of expression that suited his theory of literature, as well as a set of themes he was to reproduce in ever-varying forms. Following his first novel, he wrote *Una meditación* (A meditation, Biblioteca Breve prize, 1969) and *Un viaje de invierno* (A winter's journey, 1972), both complex developments of a convoluted series of themes. *La otra casa de Mazón* (The other house of Mazón, 1973) adds experiment in form (a combination of drama and novel) to the experimental methods of the earlier works. By setting the other works in Región, with similar treatment of themes and the same characters and locale, Benet has fashioned a hermetic universe of remarkable consistency and has gained recognition for his position as founding father of the New Novel.[42] The timeliness and originality of his contribution mark the transition to what we can accurately call " 'today' in the contemporary Spanish novel."[43]

Reivindicación del conde don Julián

By the time Juan Goytisolo published *Reivindicación del conde don Julián* (1970), he had already established a reputation as one of Spain's major novelists, and had undergone an evolution that paralleled the changing interests associated with the postwar novel: his earlier works are typical of subjective realism (*Juegos de manos*, 1954; *Duelo en el Paraíso*, 1955); an intermediate group falls into the more objective category (*La isla*, 1961). Goytisolo has also written several books of literary criticism and cultural miscellanea, useful not only as an indicator of the values of his age but also as a barometer of his own changing tastes. Particularly important is his consciousness of literary style and the values that literature and language hold in the culture they represent. Both *Problemas de la novela* (1959) and especially *El furgón de cola* (1967) are timely instruments with which to measure the New Novel.

Reivindicación is the second of a trilogy investigating personal, national, and cultural values and authenticity. The first novel, *Señas de identidad* (*Marks of Identity*, 1966), reconstructs the past of an exile who returns to Spain in search of his identity, as well as that of his homeland, and his relationship with Spain. Free association, irony, multiple stories and characters (which could be considered simply an objectification of the main character), the use of the second-person familiar form, and the identification between the protagonist and his country mark a conscious deviation from the objective reality of neorealism and initiate tendencies further developed in later works. Four years later the publication of *Reivindicación* marked the fruition of this experimentation in a landmark contribution to the New Novel in Spain.

Reivindicación is written entirely from an interior perspective, thus providing the justification for an unusually distorted reality. The protagonist leaves his rooms in Tangiers and for the space of a few hours walks the twisted streets of the city, musing about the values of his homeland, Spain, and fantasizing a new invasion based on the legend of Count Julián, an outraged father who avenged his daughter's rape by King Rodrigo by helping the Moors to invade Spain and thus causing the fall of the Visigothic reign in the eighth century. The protagonist, who identifies himself with Julián, has many encounters in his circular stroll, which triggers associations and free-form fantasies, revealing his desperate state of mind.

Associative thought clusters replace conventional plot. Snatches from his childhood, comments on life in Spain, and his own fantasies and "plans" for the new invasion form a disconnected, episodic plot, with no effort to establish cause and effect. *Reivindicación* is a Protean novel because themes and characters continually merge and metamorphose. The work is structured around recurrent and overlapping motifs, each of an introspective nature (although often set off by some actual observation or encounter) and motivated by an overall intellectual structure: the criticism of and commentary on the condition of Spain (and by implication of all Western culture) and the need for violent change and a radical break with the prevailing mentality.

In an elaboration of the theme initiated in *Señas de identidad,* the periplus of this character will encompass a dual quest: the search for authenticity of self (the return to childhood, evidenced by references to fairy tales associated with childhood) linked with the search for authentic Spain, fragmented and reiterated through dozens of subthemes and distortions. The use of the *tú* form emphasizes the theme of the double, linking the character inextricably to his homeland. The narrator acknowledges the relationship between the landscape of his journey and his inner state by saying that he will become a split personality and that he himself is a labyrinth.[44] As he emerges from the maze of Tangiers's streets, his symbolic quest ends, but only for the moment: "Sleep overwhelms your eyelids and you close your eyes: you know, you know: tomorrow will be another day, the invasion will begin again" (240). Thus, in this variation of the New Novel, plot per se and the external reality that generally informs it are completely discarded for a new type of "reality": a fluid, inner landscape that the mind can distort, reevaluate, and change at will. In accordance with the practice of the New Novel, Goytisolo develops an idea that transcends the present Spanish situation. However, while one avenue of exploration fashions a new mythology that is both universal and, in a wide sense, indicative of Spanish reality (e.g., Benet), Goytisolo takes an entirely different direction in his sarcastic, ironic attack on the historical and cultural values that form the basis of the Spanish character. Choice of subject and the ironic treatment of it are very much in the tradition of Martín-Santos:[45] both authors question the formation of the Spanish character and its cultural manifestations, using an ironic, parodic stance to convey their personal anguish. Associations with the Generation of 1898 should be obvious, particularly with the *esperpentos* of Valle-Inclán, and to some degree the observations by Baroja on Spanish character.[46]

In this more modern version of the Problem of Spain, Goytisolo takes on all of Spanish culture and finds it sadly lacking. His methodology is to select those myths and figures most cherished by Spaniards and demythologize them. Early in the novel the narrator states that he will reveal "the truth behind the mask . . . and destroy Sacred Spain" (52). The process of demythification begins in the first line, with an allusion to Spain from the point of view of the exile: "Ungrateful land, spurious and wretched among all lands, I will never return to you," thus unmistakably fixing his critical posture vis-à-vis his homeland. This major theme reappears in infinite variations: in his comments, fantasies, the reality he encounters, and the ironic lens through which all are viewed. One variation involves the presentation of individuals typically associated with Hispanic culture: Seneca, the bullfighter Manolete, Franco, and a symbolic incarnation of these values, don Alvaro Peranzules, the narrator's acquaintance in Tangiers. Their common characteristics lead to the transformation of one into the other, at times indistinguishably merging to form the idea of "The Spaniard," or, as Goytisolo sarcastically calls him, the *carpeto* (a shortened form of *carpetovetónico*, used here to signify the "pure" Spaniard), employed in *Reivindicación* as a generic term linking Spanish character with religious devotion, false pride, stoicism, pomposity, and empty rhetoric.

From the Spanish individual Goytisolo turns to literature as the crystallization and expression of a national culture: the protagonist's references to Spanish classics similarly employ irony and violence for destructive purposes. For example, the protagonist enters the library and secretly squashes insects between the pages of the great

Spanish classics (31 ff.). Constant intertextual references include borrowings from Spanish authors from medieval to present times (with a list of acknowledgments following the body of the text), most of which are subjected to ironical changes: a parody of Juan Ramón Jiménez's tender passage from the well-known *Platero y yo* (a gentle, lyrical story of a boy and a little donkey) begins, "The animal is small, shaggy, soft and he is breathing hard as if he came from very far: with one hand you will feed him while with the other you grasp the sharp knife and plunge it slowly into his throat" (147). Allusions to the lack of grandeur in the Spanish soul— symbolized by their association with the lowly *garbanzo* ("chick-pea")—end with a reference to "Garbanzote de la Mancha" (151).

Goytisolo has stated that the writer's primordial task is to be a mythoclast;[47] *Reivindicación* constitutes the practical application of this theory. In addition to his debunking notions of Spanish character, Goytisolo attacks other aspects of Spanish culture, especially Catholicism and the repressive sexual attitudes of the Spaniards. These two motifs often come together in critical context: the ascetic Holy Week procession transformed into the wildly sensuous carnival festival in Rio (74 ff.) or the scene in which Isabel the Catholic masturbates with her cross and flagellant's whip (165).[48] Parodies of Spanish religious practices and beliefs fill the book, and sexual motifs structure the work through the reiteration of phallic symbols and images of penetration (rape, invasion, and so forth). His fantasies debunk myths of childhood naiveté and fairy tales that structure behavior: fragments of "Little Red Riding Hood" appear throughout linked with the loss of innocence, treachery, incest, pederasty, and homosexuality.[49]

The reiteration of sickness as a structuring motif and symbol implies unhealthy attitudes or behavior on every level. Physical sickness appears in the obsession with two infectious diseases that are generally consequences of penetration: syphilis and rabies. Maladjustment is acknowledged in the search for self and is obviously manifested in the protagonist's shifting states of alienation, disillusionment, anger, and despair. References to ill health apply to the national level as well as the individual.

Reivindicación moves from analysis of exterior aspects of Spanish culture to scrutinize its linguistic manifestations. Language, transcending its function as medium, becomes a theme of the novel, adding a metalinguistic dimension. One of the earliest manifestations of language analysis in the Spanish New Novel, *Reivindicación* displays an affinity with international literary currents of criticism (particularly French structuralism). Language itself shapes and is shaped by the culture it transmits; no matter what Spain has lost, the Word still represents what it used to be. The equation of language with blood (196) shows its role as life force of the culture. However, according to the protagonist, the Spanish language is no longer valid, and even hides the truth of the ruin of Spain: "words, empty molds, sonorous and hollow receptacles," he states as he addresses the Spanish language and finds it at fault: "Your apparent health is a crude mirage, simony is your errand boy"; "you grow and multiply on paper, suffocating the truth behind your mask." He ends by calling for destruction: "The word has died and the headiness of action calls to you . . . violence is mute: to pillage, to destroy, to rape, to betray you will not need words" (157). The novel's syntax drastically undermines traditional modes of expression, paralleling the violence of physical invasion and the ironic parody of culture. From the first page it is obvious that Goytisolo intends to defy convention: long sections ignore customary grammatical division (sentences, periods, paragraphs, semicolons, etc.); clusters separated by colons reflect the inner landscape of connotation rather than the logic of grammar. Instead of paragraphs, lines of unequal length (sometimes only one word) are used; typographical changes or spatial rearrangements suggest free verse or concrete poetry. Official rhetoric, pat phrases, and catchwords associated with cultural or social values are revealed as empty of meaning. Examples of codified (and therefore dead) modes of expression are found in the hollow speeches of Alvaro, especially those echoing Falangist rhetoric (81), and his use of empty phrases evoking Spain's past glories to protect himself against a swarm of insects: "Come, ballad book, liturgical drama, book of chivalry: Cid the Champion, Manolete: Plateau of Spain!: mysticism, bullfighting, stoicism . . . don Alvaro's mask disinflates and wrinkles up . . . uselessly he whispers: Guadarrama, pure Soria, *me duele España* [expressions associated with the Generation of 1898's search for the essence of Spain]" (180).

Goytisolo uses incongruity to effect his destructive revisionism, repeatedly employing incongruity of language or phrase to make the reader aware of the disparity between reality and language. He uses inflated *culterano* language completely out of keeping with the situation (when he accidentally urinates on a sleeping beggar hidden in the shadows, the victim receives the "light-colored, liquid disdain" with a groan [60]). Codified modes of expression lead to exaggerated and ridiculous situations, epitomized in the trip through the genitalia of Isabel the Catholic, narrated in the official patter of a tour guide.

Images of violation and purity of blood merge with the motif of disease to affect the level of language: the novelist contaminates the "pure" Spanish lexicon with the vocabulary of their children (Spanish American terms and words [194–95]); he constantly incorporates modern terms and slang and subjects the lexicon itself to the same iconoclasm as any other manifestation of Spanish culture, stretching the language to its limit with baroque techniques and rhetorical devices, neologisms, Latinate structure, expressions, and parodic devices (for example, the classical phrase *O tempora! o mores!* becomes *o tempora! o moros!* [55]). Goytisolo constantly uses other languages for ironic or critical purposes. Finally, through one of his fantasies, he gallops through Spain, symbolically taking away the foreign words that had already contaminated the "pure" language. This foray leaves Spain hungry and on the brink of ruin, since most of these "practical" words derive from foreign sources (196 ff.).

Reivindicación obviously calls for an active reader. The ambiguity on all levels requires constant attention; the changing forms and visions draw the reader into a maze in an attempt to follow the internal logic. Tension is established through the contrast of interiorization (and thus reader identification through narrow mental images, the use of the *tú* form, and so on) with the colder, more objective stance of the parodic forms. The narrator's attraction-repulsion vis-à-vis his homeland is thus mirrored on a structural level; and the split personality of the narrations must involve the reader closely in the same kind of ambivalent feelings.

Goytisolo holds a place of preeminence in the contemporary Spanish novel. His early experimentation with language, his shifting of the author-character-reader roles, and his self-proclaimed mythoclastic function are elements that now regularly appear in Spanish literature.[50] Goytisolo has lived in Paris in self-imposed exile since 1957, although he returns to Spain often. Nevertheless, it is impossible to understand Goytisolo outside the context of his own country. Nowhere is this more true than in *Reivindicación del conde don Julián.*

Chapter Ten
España peregrina
(Spain in Exile)

An overview of contemporary Spanish literature must at least make passing reference to a phenomenon that was a direct result of the Civil War: the departure of a large number of important literary figures, the writers in exile.[1] Their absence from Spain had a profound effect on the development of literature within their homeland, breaking the literary continuum: the Mid-Century Generation, whose members would have been the natural heirs of their artistic legacy, were literary "war-orphans." Spanish critics, if familiar with the exiles' literature, ignored them, out of fear or vindictiveness.[2] The return of many of these writers to Spain several decades later can be considered a cultural landmark. During the 1960s the government instituted *operación retorno,* an effort to reintegrate the exiles into Spanish culture. Visits to their homeland, ceremonies, a flurry of publishing, and awarding of prizes were the visible results, although rediscovery of these writers has undoubtedly added a new dimension to peninsular literature.

The determining factors that molded the literature of the exiles understandably differ from those that shaped literary creativity within Spain. Their dispersal—to France, to the United States, and, particularly, to Spanish America—precluded the formation of a single, cohesive group, or sponsorship by taste-making publishing houses. Separation from their accustomed reading public intensified the writers' feeling of being cut off, unable to communicate. Francisco Ayala wrote an essay entitled "¿Para quién escribimos nosostros?" (For whom are we writing?), a poignant expression of the exile's feeling of rootlessness and lack of direction seen from the perspective of the writer in search of his public.[3]

Despite the absence of group activities and cohesiveness, and despite the mixture of generations and varying degrees of literary experience, the exiles' reaction to a common historical condition allows a certain rough grouping. One of the most thorough studies to date on exile literature, José R. Marra López's *Narrativa española fuera de España* (Spanish narrative outside Spain), develops the relationship of the exile with his homeland, which becomes a thematic constant in his literature. Memories and references to the past keep the writer in touch with his country, if only mentally. Thus many of their early novels are autobiographical in tone, treating experiential situations: childhood themes, the Civil War, their postwar circumstances in a new land. Eventually the writer reveals his diminishing commitment by a more objective stance, through abstraction and symbolism. Most other critics perceive similar thematic evolution, emphasizing the analysis of the past and the interest in the Civil War.[4] In addition, the "classical" traits attributed to many of these writers may reflect the exiles' estrangement from their situation. A more generalized identification with all people—the creation of universal or symbolic situations—may result from unconscious—or even conscious—rejection of the present circumstances.

The most famous and translated exile, Ramón J. Sender, has written a series of poignant fictional memoirs, *Crónica del alba* (Chronicle of the dawn, 1942–67, published as *Before Noon*), nine volumes of the writings of Pepe Garcés, from childhood through the Civil War, structured by news of his death in a "preface" to the first volume. Later works, less autobiographical, intertwine realism and symbolism (for example, the Civil War theme in *El rey y la reina* [*The King and the Queen,* 1949] or *Mossén Millán,* 1953). Sender's commentaries on human nature are often allegorical (*El verdugo afable* [*The Affable Hangman,* 1952] or his reworking of Calderón de la Barca's *La vida es sueño: Los laureles de Anselmo* [The laurels of Anselmo, 1958]). A series of historical novels (for example, *La aventura equinoccial de Lope de Aguirre* [The equinoctial adventure of Lope de Aguirre]) contrasts human emotions and ambitions with the official versions of events. A magic dimension (present in early works such as *Epitalamio del prieto Trinidad* [*Dark Wedding,* 1942], the story of an unusual rebellion in a South American penal colony), becomes more pronounced in later novels like *El fugitivo* (The fugitive, 1976). Sender's return to Spain was met with great fanfare, and he received several important literary prizes. His death in 1982 was a loss to the international world of letters.

Francisco Ayala is likewise of major importance among the exiled writers. His work underwent an evolution from the highly intellectual, metaphoric prose of prewar years to a more humanistic perspective, combining specific plot with universal implications. Two highly acclaimed novels, *Muertes de perro* (Dog's death, published as *Death as a Way of Life*, 1958) and *El fondo del vaso* (The bottom of the glass, 1962), explore the characteristics of a Spanish American dictatorship within the wider context of patterns of human behavior. A prize-winning work, *El jardín de las delicias* (The garden of delights, 1971), employs an experimental narrator, while counterpoint and fragmentation (a transference of Bosch's artistic techniques to the printed page) offer new perspectives from which to view mankind.

Another place of importance belongs to Max Aub, whose series of novels, collectively entitled *El laberinto mágico* (The magic labyrinth), chronicles historical and personal circumstances surrounding the Civil War. Obviously, the extensive list of exiled authors prevents giving each his due recognition, but at least four others deserve mention. Arturo Barea won international attention for his best-selling autobiographical trilogy *The Forging of a Rebel* (1941). Manuel Andújar's trilogy *Vísperas* (On the eve, 1970) combines historical and social determinants as they affect the common man in prewar Spain; Segundo Serrano Poncela's *El hombre de la cruz verde* (The man with the green cross, 1969) studies the epoch of Felipe II. Rosa Chacel's novels of retrospection, including *Memorias de Leticia Valle* (Memoirs of Leticia Valle, 1945) and *La sinrazón* (The wrong, 1960), retain characteristics of the "dehumanized novel" cultivated during the prewar period and later adapted in the New Novel.

As exile literature has begun to receive greater attention, critics have realized the inherent difficulties in categorizing all exiles within a single group. One attempt at reevaluation divides exiled authors into four types: (1) authors who published in Spain before the Civil War and left after the war (Sender, Ayala); (2) a second group who left Spain in 1939 as children; (3) those authors who published after 1950 both in Spain and abroad (Juan Goytisolo); and (4) "exiled works"—books published abroad by writers who live in Spain.[5]

While the traditional conception of exile status implies geographical distance and persecution, Paul Ilie's recent study suggests that exile can also be a state of mind. In *Literature and Inner Exile,* he develops the notion of residential exile in addition to territorial exile.[6] Alienation, frustration, mental deprivation, and a sense of failure also characterize the attitudes of some who remained in Spain, an "expatriated" mentality that appears in the reiteration of themes such as rootlessness (the travel literature, for example) and the prisoner theme. Repression thus engenders a literature that depicts exile no matter what the geographical location of the writer.

Chapter Eleven
Conclusions

Extraliterary factors weighed heavily in determining the direction of postwar Spanish literature. Realism was the main choice of most writers working under the Franco regime, although reasons for this choice varied somewhat.

Certain manifestations of neorealism make as strong a political statement as was possible during a period of such restrictive policies. Compensating for the lack of freedom to criticize explicitly, the writers present "facts"—situations, details, settings, and relationships—that make the reader an eyewitness to the problems of contemporary conditions. Exposés of this type tend to concentrate on the subject matter itself; style and technique are important only as communicative devices. Experimental techniques are occasionally evident as subtle means of conveying underlying objections or criticism: both subjective and objectivist neorealism used style or form to transmit a less "objective" sense of the situation, attempting to draw the reader more closely into the story through affective devices.

Not until the more innovative directions of Martín-Santos and the New Novel do writers discard neorealism of the social and objectivist variety for experimentation with form and the presentation of a different type of reality. Critical intentions remain the same, but a change is noticeable in the author's undisguisedly subjective and intellectual position. Exploration of cultural values (including language and fiction itself) and other dimensions of reality mark the change in direction, which includes a different relationship between the reader and the text. Directly related to these new forms is the relaxation of censorship policies and the greater contact between Spain and the outside world.

In the last years of Franco's reign and the years following his death, the novel has moved rapidly through various phases: more controversial subject matter has not unexpectedly appeared after so many years of silence. The following decades will be more indicative of Spain's real artistic capabilities, since freedom of expression and a receptive public have replaced control and disapproval. The Spanish novel can once again take its place in international fiction, where the unrestricted creativity of contemporary writers may restore to it the prestige of its remarkable heritage.

Notes and References

Chapter One

1. See, for example, the remarks of Ricardo Doménech in "Una generación en marcha," *Insula* 15 (June 1970):5.

2. For an interesting summary of Falangist cultural and literary attitudes during the war years, see the articles entitled "A Falangist View of Golden Age Literature" (pp. 182–90), "A Fascist View of Nineteenth-Century Spanish Literature (1936–1939)" (pp. 191–96), "Culture and the Spanish Civil War—A Fascist View: 1936–1939" (pp. 197–218) reprinted from various journals in Kessel Schwartz's *The Meaning of Existence in Contemporary Hispanic Literature* (Coral Gables: University of Miami Press, 1969).

3. Eugenio G. de Nora, *La novela española contemporánea (1939–1967)*, 2d ed. ampliada (Madrid: Editorial Gredos, 1979), 3:47.

4. Much of the information concerning censorship in Spain comes from Manuel L. Abellán, *Censura y creación literaria en España (1939–1976)* (Barcelona: Ediciones Península, 1980).

5. Ana María Matute, "The Short Story in Spain," trans. William Fifield, *Kenyon Review* 31, no. 126 (1969):453.

6. Santos Sanz Villanueva, *Historia de la novela social española (1942–1975)* (Madrid, 1980), insists on this fact in a chapter entitled "Los años cuarenta," 1:19–57. For a brief discussion of this aspect of censorship, as well as the types of foreign novels published at this time, see Fernando Alvarez Palacios's *Novela y cultura española de postguerra* (Madrid, 1975), pp. 15–22.

7. Carmen Martín Gaite, "Un aviso: ha muerto Ignacio Aldecoa," in *La búsqueda de interlocutor y otras búsquedas* (Madrid: Nostromo, 1973), pp. 34–35.

8. Gonzalo Torrente Ballester, in *Novela española actual* (Madrid: Fundación Juan March y Ediciones Cátedra, 1977), p. 113.

9. For some discussion of the purpose and relative value of these prizes, see Alvarez Palacios, *Novela,* pp. 23–31, and J. M. Martínez-Cachero, *La novela española entre 1939 y 1975* (Madrid: Editorial Castalia, 1979), pp. 245–50.

Chapter Two

1. Galdós was not alone in the development of the modern historical novel. Baroja's twenty-two volumes collectively entitled *Memorias de un*

hombre de acción are an excellent example of a single individual's (Eugenio de Aviraneta, a nineteenth-century figure) interacting with historical circumstances. For further examples not employed in traditional realism, see Madeleine de Gogorza Fletcher, *The Spanish Historical Novel (1880–1970)* (London: Tamesis, 1973).

2. Martínez-Cachero, *La novela,* p. 120.

3. Ignacio Agustí, *Mariona Rebull,* 9th ed. (Barcelona, 1953), p. 9. Quotations in the text are from this edition.

4. Juan A. de Zunzunegui, *La vida como es* (Barcelona, 1954), p. 208. Quotations in the text come from this edition.

5. Of course, many minor works are also considered truly picaresque, or at least display many of the basic characteristics. See Betty Rita Gómez Lance, *La actitud picaresca en la novela española siglo XX* (Mexico: B. Costa-Amic, 1968).

6. Ibid., p. 128.

Chapter Three

1. A remark repeated by several critics, among them Juan Luis Alborg, *Hora actual de la novela española* (Madrid: Taurus, 1958), 1:87.

2. Camilo José Cela, "Sobre los tremendismos," in *La rueda de los ocios* (Barcelona: Editorial Mateu, 1962), pp. 13–16.

3. I will use the terms "story" (i.e., raw chronological materials) and "plot" (narrative as actually shaped) following the definition of Robert Scholes, "The Contributions of Formalism and Structuralism to the Theory of Fiction," *Novel* 6 (Winter 1973):134–51.

4. The relationship between the aesthetics of *tremendismo* and the general atmosphere of postwar Spain is a constant factor in critical studies, for example Nora, *La novela,* pp. 70–71, or Robert C. Spires, *La novela española de posguerra: creación artística y experiencia personal* (Madrid, 1978). Later, the cumulative impression of the misery of a specific sector was one of the adaptations of *tremendismo* to the social novel.

5. Luis López Molina, "El tremendismo en la literatura española actual," *Revista de Occidente* 18, no. 54 (1967), describes some of the excesses on pp. 375–76.

6. Early explorations of these tendencies in modern Spanish literature may be seen in Olga P. Ferrer, "La literatura española tremendista y su nexo con el existencialismo," *Revista hispánica moderna* 22 (July-October 1956):297–303, and Julian Palley, "Existentialist Trends in the Modern Spanish Novel," *Hispania* 44 (March 1961):21–26. For a more extensive study of existentialism in the contemporary Spanish novel as well as a brief analysis of the points of intersection of this philosophy and *tremendismo,* see Gemma Roberts, *Temas existenciales en la novela española de postguerra* (Madrid: Gredos, 1973).

7. A theory expounded by Julián Marías in "Presencia y ausencia del existencialismo en España," in *Obras* (Madrid: Revista de Occidente, 1969), 5:233–47.

8. Camilo José Cela, *La familia de Pascual Duarte*, ed. Harold L. Boudreau and John W. Kronik (New York, 1961), p. 11. Quotations in the text are from this edition.

9. Several critics have commented on the various narrators in the novel and the implicit or explicit contradictions arising from conflicting evidence. See, among others, Robert C. Spires, "Systematic Doubt: The Moral Art of *La familia de Pascual Duarte*," *Hispanic Review* 3 (Summer 1972):283–302; Dru Dougherty, "Pascual en la cárcel: el encubierto relato de *La familia de Pascual Duarte*," *Insula* 32, no. 365 (April 1977):5, 7; Agnes M. Gullón, "La transcripción de *La familia de Pascual Duarte*," *Insula* 33, no. 377 (April 1978):1, 10.

10. For an elaboration on this theme, consult Cedric Busette, *"La familia de Pascual Duarte* and the Prominence of Fate," *Revista de estudios hispánicos* 8, no. 1 (January 1974):61–67.

11. D. W. McPheeters, *Camilo José Cela* (Boston: Twayne Publishers, 1969) discusses the pros and cons of *tremendismo* and existentialism in this novel and provides a bibliography on the subject.

12. Robert C. Spires, "La dinámica tonal de *La familia de Pascual Duarte*," in *La novela española de posguerra*, pp. 24–51.

13. Carmen Leforet, *Nada*, 13th ed. (Barcelona, 1960), p. 17. Quotations in the text are from this edition.

14. Two excellent studies of rites of passage in *Nada* are contained in Juan Villegas's "*Nada* de Carmen Laforet o la infantilización de la aventura legendaria," in *La estructura mítica del héroe* (Barcelona: Planeta, 1973), pp. 177–201, and Michael D. Thomas, "Symbolic Portals in Laforet's *Nada*," *Anales de la novela de posguerra* 3 (1978):57–74. A thorough study-cum-bibliography of Laforet's works may be found in Roberta Johnson's *Carmen Laforet* (Boston: Twayne Publishers, 1981).

Chapter Four

1. For a thorough discussion of the various ways of grouping this and other postwar generations, see Sanz Villanueva, *Historia de la novela social española*, 1:67–79.

2. The thesis presented by Fernando Morán in his *Explicación de una limitación: la novela realista de los años cincuenta en España* (Madrid, 1971), p. 74.

3. Sanz Villanueva, *Historia de la novela social española*, 1:12.

4. Juan Goytisolo, "Literatura y eutenasia," in *El furgón de cola* (Paris: Ruedo Ibérico, 1967), p. 46, and José María Castellet, "La joven novela española," *Sur*, no. 284 (1963):51.

5. Quoted in Antonio Núñez, "Encuentro con Ana María Matute," *Insula* 20 (February 1965):7.

6. For descriptions of the various journals, see Laureano Bonet, "La revista 'Laye' y la novela de los años cincuenta," *Insula* 34 (November-December 1979):8, and Darío Villanueva's introduction for the connection between the Mid-Century Generation and the *Revista española* in *El Jarama de Sánchez Ferlosio: su estructura y significado* (Santiago, 1973).

7. Juan Goytisolo, "Los escritores españoles frente al toro de la censura," in *El furgón de cola*, p. 34.

8. Morán, *Explicación*, p. 58.

9. Doménech, for example, laments the fact that the Generation of 1898 was so neglected: "Una generación en marcha," p. 5. There is mixed critical opinion concerning Baroja's influence. See Sanz Villanueva's discussion in his *Historia de la novela social española*, 1:125–26. Manuel Alvar, "Noventa y ocho y la novela de posguerra," in *Novelistas españoles de postguerra*, ed. Rodolfo Cardona (Madrid: Taurus, 1976), pp. 13–16, traces influences in the novel up to 1955.

10. Darío Villanueva, *El Jarama*, p. 24.

11. José María Castellet, *La hora del lector* (Barcelona: Seix Barral, 1957).

12. Juan Goytisolo, *Problemas de la novela* (Barcelona: Seix Barral, 1959), p. 16. Goytisolo later repudiated this position.

13. Juan Goytisolo, "Para una literatura nacional," *Insula* 146 (January 1959):6, 22.

14. Castellet, *La hora del lector*, p. 101.

Chapter Five

1. Evidence of interest in phenomonology, psychology, etc., are found in Evelyne López Campillo, *La Revista de Occidente y la formación de minorías (1923–1936)* (Madrid: Taurus, 1972).

2. Darío Villanueva, *El Jarama*, does not see any marked influence of the "nouveau roman" until García Hortelano.

3. For a discussion of this subject, see Manuel Alvar, "Técnica cinematográfica en la novela española de hoy," *Arbor* 71, no. 276 (December 1968):253–70.

4. Juan García Hortelano, cited in Federico Campbell, *Infame turba* (Barcelona: Lumen, 1971), p. 262.

5. One of the early studies dealing with this aspect appears in José Francisco Cirre, "El protagonista múltiple y su papel en la reciente novela española," *Papeles de Son Armadans* 33, no. 98 (May 1964):159–70.

6. A point of view evident in Goytisolo's *Problemas de la novela*.

7. Juan García Hortelano, cited in Campbell, *Infame turba*, p. 263.

8. The reader interested in further exploration of general critical analyses of objectivism should consult Janet Winecoff, "The Spanish Novel from Ortega to Castellet: Dehumanization of the Artist," *Hispania* 50, no. 1 (March 1967):35–43; Ramón Buckley, "La objetividad como meta," in *Teoría de la novela,* ed. Santos Sanz Villanueva and Carlos J. Barbachano (Madrid: Sociedad General Española de Librería, 1976), pp. 265–89; or Buckley's chapter entitled "Objetivismo," in *Problemas formales de la novela contemporánea* (Barcelona, 1968), pp. 37–77; Antonio Vilanova, "De la objetividad al subjetivismo en la novela española actual," *Prosa novelesca actual* (Santander: Universidad Menéndez Pelayo, 1968), pp. 133–56. To balance the introduction, read the objections of Ricardo Doménech, "Una reflexión sobre el objetivismo," *Insula* 180 (November 1961):6, or Guillermo de Torre, in his chapter on objectivism in *Historia de las literaturas de vanguardia* (Madrid: Guadarrama, 1965).

9. Camilo José Cela, *La colmena,* 8th ed. (Madrid, 1967). Quotations in the text come from this edition.

10. For Cela's remarks concerning censorship, publication, and subsequent reactions to *La colmena,* see his "Historia incompleta de unas páginas zarandeadas," in *Obras completas* (Barcelona: Editorial Destino, 1969), 7:37–46.

11. One earlier experiment using multiple characters and simultaneity of action was written by José Suárez Carreño. *Las últimas horas* won the Nadal Prize in 1949 but was not as influential as *La colmena.* See José Corrales Egea, *La novela española actual* (Madrid, 1971), pp. 54–55, for some explanations as to why this novel is not considered as important as *La colmena.*

12. According to C[aballero] B[onald], in his "censo de personajes," following the text of the edition cited above.

13. Nora, *La novela,* p. 120.

14. Cela, *Obras completas,* 7:976.

15. Most critics agree that, although there are connections with social criticism, *La colmena* cannot be considered a true social novel (see Pablo Gil Casado, *La novela social española,* 2d ed. [Barcelona, 1973], pp. 111–13, or Sanz Villanueva, *Historia de la novela social española,* 1:270–74.)

16. An opinion that appears in many of Cela's works. See, for example the section on travel literature (p. 65) for another version.

17. See José Ortega, "Símiles de animalidad en *La Colmena,*" *Romance Notes* 8 (1966):6–10.

18. In the note to the first edition (p. 9) and to the fourth (p. 15).

19. Camilo José Cela, *Tobogán de hambrientos,* 2d ed. (Barcelona: Noguer, 1964).

20. Other studies on *La colmena* include chapter 6 in McPheeters's *Camilo José Cela*, which includes a bibliography, and David Henn, *La colmena* (London: Grant and Cutler, 1974).

21. Nora, *La novela*, p. 312.

22. Jesús Fernández Santos, *Los bravos* (Valencia, 1954). All quotations in the text come from this edition.

23. When questioned about his "objective realism" Fernández Santos replied that the limitation of censorship concerning direct opinions eventually became a style. David K. Herzberger, "Entrevista con Jesús Fernández Santos," *Anales de la novela de posguerra* 3 (1978):117–21.

24. For example, a study of one region alone chronicles migration patterns from Andalusia: ". . . the uncontrolled flight of its inhabitants—not just a transfer of population from agriculture to industry and services, but the depopulation of entire villages and towns." John Naylon, *Andalusia* (London: Oxford University Press, 1975), p. 22.

25. Gil Casado, *La novela social española*, pp. 244–45, offers a different interpretation. He considers Prudencio a petty tyrant; at his death, the doctor "can begin to exercise his tyranny over the little town. . . ."

26. Those who wish to consult more extensive studies of *Los bravos* (in addition to the above references and the brief analyses in various critical studies cited in the bibliography) may consult Alborg, *Hora actual de la novela española*, 2:373–78; Juan Carlos Curutchet, "La indagación esencial de Jesús Fernández Santos," in his *Introducción a la novela española de postguerra* (Montevideo: Editorial Alfa, 1966), pp. 97–118; Sanz Villanueva, *Historia de la novela social española*, 1:344–41; Michael D. Thomas, "Penetrando la superficie: apuntes sobre la estructura narrativa de *Los bravos*," *Anales de la narrativa española contemporánea* 5 (1980):83–90. David K. Herzberger traces this author's literary development in *Jesús Fernández Santos* (Boston: Twayne Publishers, 1983).

27. Rafael Sánchez Ferlosio, *El Jarama*, 8th ed. (Barcelona, 1967). Quotations in the text come from this edition.

28. Alborg, *Hora actual de la novela española*, 1:329 ff.

29. The linguistic aspect has been noted in an excellent study by Darío Villanueva, *El Jarama*, pp. 111–23, and in Buckley, *Problemas formales*, pp. 65–68.

30. A fact noted by many critics; for example, Antonio Risco, "Una relectura de *El Jarama* de Sánchez Ferlosio," *Cuadernos hispanoamericanos* 288 (June 1974):702.

31. Buckley, *Problemas formales*, p. 73.

32. Edward C. Riley, "Sobre el arte de Sánchez Ferlosio: aspectos de *El Jarama*," a "corrected" version of an article first appearing in *Filología* 9 (1963):201–21, and included in Cardona, *Novelistas españoles de postguerra*, pp. 123–41.

33. Buckley's discussion of Sánchez Ferlosio's "presence" in *El Jarama* is most interesting (*Problemas formales*, pp. 67–77).

34. Morán, *Explicación*, pp. 20–55.

35. A criticism that one critic sees in the novel, linking this to a wider spiritual crisis in society generally. José Ortega, "Tiempo y estructura en *El Jarama*," *Cuadernos hispanoamericanos* 201 (September 1966):801–8.

36. Buckley, "La objetividad como meta," p. 275.

37. Morán, *Explicación*, pp. 81–85.

38. Darío Villanueva discusses these characteristics: *El Jarama*, pp. 131–34.

39. Edward C. Riley correctly suggests that once the tragic ending has been revealed, a rereading endows the novel with an entirely different perspective.

40. A perceptive point in an excellent article by F. García Sarriá, "*El Jarama*. Muerte y merienda de Lucita," *Bulletin of Hispanic Studies* 53, no. 4 (October 1976):323–37.

41. Darío Villanueva, *El Jarama*, pp. 148–49, provides evidence for this interpretation, as does Riley, "Sobre el arte."

42. J. Schraibman and W. T. Little, "La estructura simbólica de *El Jarama*," *Philological Quarterly* 51, no. 1 (January 1972):329–42. Darío Villanueva also sees considerable evidence of authorial participation, principally in point of view.

43. Darío Villanueva, *El Jarama*, pp. 150–51.

Chapter Six

1. Sanz Villanueva, *El Jarama*, 1:174, widens the parameters considerably. In his list of writers of social realism he includes Juan Goytisolo, Francisco Candel, Luis Goytisolo, Jesús López Pacheco, Lauro Olmo, Juan José Poblador, Antonio Ferres, Juan García Hortelano, Ramón Nieto, Armando López Salinas, Juan Marsé, Daniel Sueiro, Fernando Avalos, José María Castillo Navarro, Jorge Ferrer-Vidal, Alfonso Grosso, Nino Quevedo, José Manuel Caballero Bonald, Isaac Montero, Juan Antonio Payno, Luis Martín-Santos, Mauro Muñiz, Rodrigo Rubio, José Antonio Vizcaíno, José Antonio Parra, Fidel Vela, Juan Jesús Rodero, Isabel Alvarez de Toledo, Antonio García Cano, José María Alvarez Cruz, Ignacio Aldecoa, Fernández Santos, Sánchez Ferlosio, and Martín Gaite.

2. The thesis of Morán in his *Explicación*.

3. A point made by A. Martínez Menchen, *Del desengaño literario* (Madrid: Editorial Helios, 1970), pp. 102–3. This was, according to him, one of its failings.

4. José Díaz Fernández, *El nuevo Romanticismo* (Madrid: Editorial Zeus, 1930).

5. Goytisolo, "Literatura y eutanesia," p. 49.

6. Gil Casado, *La novela social*, p. 121, states that Lukacs and Brecht were discovered "tardíamente." José María Castellet, in "Mesa redonda: la literatura social," *Camp de l'arpa*, 1 May 1972, pp. 14–18, sees the influence of Lukacs (citing *Central eléctrica* as an example), Brecht, Marx, and Engels.

7. José María Castellet reports on the conference in "Coloquio internacional sobre Novela en Formentor," *Cuadernos del congreso por la libertad de la cultura* 38 (September-October 1959):86.

8. As keenly analyzed by Sanz Villanueva, *Historia de la novela social española*, 1:83.

9. García Hortelano, for example, remarked that more of his works were sold abroad than in his own country. In E. García Rico, *Literatura y política: en torno al realismo social* (Madrid: Ed. Cuadernos del diálogo, 1971), p. 14.

10. Sanz Villanueva, *Historia de la novela social española*, 1:163, disagrees, stating that the intention is documentary rather than *costumbrista*.

11. Gil Casado, *La novela social*, devotes an entire section to "La vivienda," pp. 371–91.

12. Armando López Salinas, *La mina* (Barcelona, 1960), p. 37.

13. Gil Casado, *La novela social*, describes at some length the representative character, including some of the criticism.

14. Morán, *Explicación*, p. 58, treats this idea in the conflict between generations.

15. Martínez Menchen, *Del desengaño literario*, pp. 111–12, characterizes the dolce vita aspects as escape literature.

16. See Sanz Villanueva, *Historia de la novela social española*, 1:210–11.

17. Martínez Menchen gives this and other examples in his description of the demise of social realism: *Del desengño literario*, p. 97.

18. For some examples, see J. M. Martínez Cachero, *La novela española entre 1936 y 1969* (Madrid, 1973), pp. 230 ff., for a chapter detailing negative reactions to social literature.

19. See Ricardo Doménech's remarks in "Ante una novela irrepitible," *Insula* 187 (June 1962):4, or Eugenio G. de Nora's comments in a panel discussion held for *Insula* 205 (December 1963):3.

20. Martínez Menchen, *Del desengaño literario*, p. 104.

21. Armando López Salinas, *La mina* (Barcelona, 1960). All quotations are taken from this edition.

22. Gil Casado, *La novela social*, p. 347, states that the crowd attacks the Administrative Office (about two and a half pages that were excised in the Spanish editions) and that, as protest, the workers did not show up at work at the time of the shift change.

23. One critic, however, notes that this ending, with its hopeful note, "does not come from the action itself . . . , but from a confidence that is not explained in a literary sense and whose hidden basis is found in the ideology of the author, which makes him participate in the belief in a better future" (Sanz Villanueva, *Historia de la novela social española,* 2:576).

24. J. M. Caballero Bonald, *Dos días de setiembre,* 2d ed. (Barcelona, 1967). Quotations in the text come from this edition.

25. Juan Carlos Curutchet, in *Cuatro ensayos sobre la nueva novela española* (Montevideo: Editorial Alfa, S.A., 1973), p. 20, says that the town is Jérez de la Frontera.

26. Interview in Francisco Olmos García, "La novela y los novelistas españoles de hoy," *Cuadernos americanos* 22, no. 4 (July-August 1963):214.

27. Robert Kirsner, for example, calls Cela's travel literature "quasi novels, . . . fundamentally lyrical novels in which the author brings together fact and fantasy." *The Novels and Travels of Camilo José Cela* (Chapel Hill: University of North Carolina Press, 1964), pp. 100–101.

28. Camilo J. Cela, *Viaje a la Alcarria,* 3d ed. (Madrid, 1961). All quotations in the text come from this edition.

29. In a revealing statement taken from his dedication, Cela writes, "Anything goes in a novel, as long as it's told with common sense, but in geography, as is natural, that no longer is the case and it is necessary to tell the truth always, because it is like a science" (p. 14).

30. Sanz Villanueva, *Historia de la novela social española,* 2:778.

31. Antonio Ferres and Armando López Salinas, *Caminando por las Hurdes* (Barcelona: Seix Barral, 1960), p. 9.

32. For further information on travel literature, see Sanz Villanueva, *Historia de la novela social española,* 1:193–97, for a brief discussion of some of the lesser-known writers. This aspect of Cela and others will be found in the sections dealing with individual authors. For an interesting interpretation of Cela's point of view in writing this type of literature, see Paul Ilie, "Primitivismo y vagabundaje en la obra de C. J. Cela," *Insula* 16, no. 170 (January 1961):14, or Gil Casado, chapter 6 of his *Novela social española.*

Chapter Seven

1. M. García Viñó, *Novela española de posguerra* (Madrid, 1971), p. 54.

2. The subject of young people as protagonists in the novels of the Mid-Century Generation is constantly mentioned in critical histories (for example, Juan Carlos Curutchet, *Introducción a la novela española de postguerra,* p.60 ff.) and has been treated in depth in studies analyzing individual authors. Overviews may be seen in Phyllis Zatlin Boring, "The

World of Childhood in the Contemporary Spanish Novel," *Kentucky Romance Quarterly* 23 (1976):467–81, or Eduardo Godoy Gallardo, *La infancia en la narrativa española de posguerra* (Madrid: Playor, 1979). Various papers on the subject are contained in the Proceedings of the Fourth Annual Conference on Hispanic Literatures, *El niño en las literaturas hispánicas,* ed. J. Cruz Mendizabal (Indiana: Indiana University of Pennsylvania, 1978), vol. 2. The subject arises in interviews, too: several writers comment on the meaning of childhood in their works in Olmos García, *La novela y los novelistas de hoy,* pp. 229–31.

    3. There is a lengthy bibliography on literary interpretations of the Spanish Civil War. Two book-length studies are José Vila Selma, *Tres ensayos sobre la literatura y nuestra guerra* (Madrid: Editorial Nacional, 1956), and José Luis S. Ponce de León, *La novela española de la guerra civil (1936– 1939)* (Madrid: *Insula,* 1971). Bibliographical articles are also available; for example, Maryse Bertrand de Muñoz, "Bibliografía de la novela de la guerra civil española," *La Torre* 16 (July-September 1968):215–42, and 17 (October-December 1969):119–30. A more recent bibliography is Malcolm Alan Compitello's "The Novel, the Critics and the Civil War: A Bibliographic Essay," *Anales de la narrativa española contemporánea* 4 (1979):117–38.

    4. Buckley, *Problemas formales,* mentions some mythical aspects in his chapter on Goytisolo, particularly pp. 162 ff.

    5. Ana María Matute, *Fiesta al noroeste,* 3d ed. (Barcelona, 1963), p. 9. Quotations in the text come from this edition.

    6. Margaret E. W. Jones, "Antipathetic Fallacy: The Hostile World of Ana María Matute's Novels," *Kentucky Foreign Language Quarterly* 13 (Supplement, 1967):5–16, offers a study of this technique in relation to nature.

    7. Gonzalo Sobejano, *Novela española de nuestro tiempo,* 2d ed. (Madrid, 1970), p. 349.

    8. M. García Viñó, "La nueva novela española," in *La nueva novela europea* (Madrid: Ediciones Guadarrama, 1968), p. 52.

    9. Ignacio Soldevila Durante pays tribute to the differing concerns even within the realistic tendencies of the Mid-Century Generation in the section entitled "Novela testimonial de talante existencial-cristiano," pp. 313–23 in his *La Novela desde 1936* (Madrid: Alhambra, 1980). For the connection between existentialism and the contemporary Spanish novel, see Roberts, *Temas existenciales en la novela española de postguerra.*

    10. Ana María Matute, *Primera memoria* (Barcelona, 1960), p. 20. Quotations in the text come from this edition.

    11. Two works that present an overview of Matute's novelistic production may be seen in Margaret E. W. Jones, *The Literary World of Ana*

María Matute (Lexington: University Press of Kentucky, 1970); and Janet W. Díaz, *Ana María Matute* (Boston: Twayne Publishers, 1971).

12. Miguel Delibes, *Cinco horas con Mario,* 4th ed. (Barcelona, 1969). Quotations in the text come from this edition.

13. One interesting study of language may be seen in Agnes M. Gullón, "Descifrando los silencios de ayer: *Cinco horas con Mario,*" *Insula* 34 (November-December 1979):4.

14. For example, Gonzalo Sobejano, who considers Carmen as an example of both Spanish woman and traditional Spain: "Los poderes de Antonia Quijana (Sobre *Cinco horas con Mario* de Miguel Delibes)," *Revista hispánica moderna* 35, nos. 1–2 (January-April 1969):106–12.

15. A perceptive study of the uses of the ironical mode may be seen in H. L. Boudreau, "*Cinco horas con Mario* and the Dynamics of Irony," *Anales de la novela de posguerra* 2 (1977):7–17.

16. Readers interested in further study of this and other works by Delibes may consult Janet W. Díaz, *Miguel Delibes* (Boston: Twayne Publishers, 1971).

Chapter Eight

1. Luis Martín-Santos, *Tiempo de silencio,* 6th ed. (Barcelona, 1969). Quotations in the text come from this edition.

2. See, for example, Ricardo Doménech's remarks concerning the fact that "he did not find the reception that he doubtless deserved," in "Luis Martín-Santos," *Insula* 19, no. 208 (March 1964):4.

3. Ricardo Doménech, "Ante una novela irrepetible," *Insula* 187 (June 1962):4.

4. Fernando Morán, *Novela y semidesarrollo* (Madrid, 1971), p. 317.

5. For remarks attributed to Martín-Santos, either directly or indirectly, see Janet Winecoff Díaz, "Luis Martín-Santos and the Contemporary Spanish Novel," *Hispania* 51, no. 2 (May 1968):232–38; Doménech, "Luis Martín-Santos," p. 4, and Aquilino Duque, "Un buen entendedor de la realidad: Luis Martín-Santos," *Indice* 17, no. 185 (June 1964):9–10.

6. Winecoff Díaz, "Luis Martín-Santos," p. 235.

7. Ibid., p. 237.

8. Martín-Santos was the director of a psychiatric hospital in San Sebastián from 1961 to 1964 and published two studies in existential psychology: *Dilthey, Jaspers y la comprensión del enfermo mental* (1955) and *Libertad, temporalidad y transferencia en el psicoanálisis existencial* (1964).

9. Several articles treat the psychoanalytic aspects of the novel. Some examples may be consulted in Robert C. Spires, who discusses the progressive integration of the authentic being in the narrative person: "Otro tú, yo: la creación y destrucción del ser auténtico en *Timepo de silencio,*"

Kentucky Romance Quarterly 22 (1975):91–110; in the Freudian approach of Carlos Feal Deibe's "Consideraciones psicoanalíticas sobre *Tiempo de silencio* de Luis Martín-Santos," *Revista hispánica moderna* 36, no. 3 (1970–71):118–27, or the wider context of Joseph Schraibman: *"Tiempo de silencio* y la cura psiquiátrica de un pueblo: España," *Insula* 32, no. 365 (April 1977):3.

10. Roberts, *Temas existenciales,* p. 190, makes this statement in a chapter devoted to the existential aspects of *Tiempo de silencio.*

11. José Ortega speaks of this in "Realismo dialéctico de Martín-Santos en *Tiempo de silencio," Revista de estudios hispánicos* 3, no. 1 (1969):33–42. He mentions the debunking role of the novelist in the Winecoff-Díaz interview (p. 237): "[The function of the novelist in society] is *desacralizadora* ["de-sacralizing"]—he destroys via a sharp criticism of what is unjust [and his function is also] sacrogenetic—at the same time he collaborates in the construction of the new myths that go on to form the Holy Scriptures of the future."

12. Alfonso Rey, *Construcción y sentido de Tiempo de silencio* (Madrid: Ediciones José Porrúa Turranzas, 1977), pp. 58–63, uses this image in a perceptive study of metonymy.

13. The theme of sex and instinct has been approached in various ways. The Freudian point of view, with emphasis on mother-relationship, the incest theme, and the "terrible mother," may be seen in Feal Deibe's article (note 9), and in Betty Jean Craige, *"Tiempo de silencio:* 'Le Grand Bouc' and the Maestro," *Revista de estudios hispánicos* 13 (1979):99–113.

14. Critics are divided as to the provenance of some of the voices, a testimony to the deliberate ambiguity. Felisa Heller, for example, asks if the diatribe in the Goya section belongs to Pedro the protagonist or Pedro the narrator: "Voz narrativa y protagonista en *Tiempo de silencio," Anales de la novela de posguerra* 3 (1978):27–37. Walter Holzinger, *"Tiempo de silencio:* An Analysis," *Revista Hispánica Moderna* 37, nos. 1–2 (1972–73):73–90, states that the narrator is a separate entity.

15. Juan Carlos Curutchet, "Luis Martín-Santos, El Fundador, I," *Cuadernos de Ruedo Ibérico,* no. 17 (February–March 1968):4.

16. A point made by Morán, *Novela y semidesarrollo,* pp. 385–86.

17. Villegas, *La estructura mítica del héroe,* pp. 203–30, and Julian Palley, "The Periplus of don Pedro: *Tiempo de silencio," Bulletin of Hispanic Studies* 48 (July 1971):239–54, are two examples of the application of mythic patterns.

18. A term aptly applied by Curutchet, "Luis Martín-Santos, El Fundador, I," p. 3.

Chapter Nine

1. M. García Viñó's *Novela española actual* (Madrid, 1967) was an early attempt to signal works beyond the purview of social or documentary realism.

2. In an attempt to make a chronological scheme, José Domingo divides the writers into "Novísimos, nuevos y renovados," *Insula* 28 (March 1973):6.

3. The thesis of Morán in *Novela y semidesarrollo*.

4. J. M. Martínez Cachero dedicates a few pages to "Otras novelas distintas," in *La novela española entre 1939 y 1969,* pp. 116–19.

5. The term used by Alvarez Palacios, *Novela y cultura española de postguerra,* p. 356.

6. Alvarez Palacio's chapter on "Los latinoamericanos," ibid., is a good example of this attitude.

7. A remark by Gonzalo Torrente Ballester in Andrés Amorós, "Conversación con Gonzalo Torrente Ballester sobre *La Saga/fuga de J. B.,*" *Insula* 28 (April 1973):4.

8. David K. Herzberger analyses this element in Benet: "Enigma as Narrative Determinant in the Novels of Juan Benet," *Hispanic Review* 47 (1979):149–57.

9. Jesús López Pacheco, *La hoja de parra* (Mexico: Joaquín Mortiz, 1973), p. 117. Quotations in the text come from this edition.

10. J. M. Caballero Bonald, *Agata, ojo de gato* (Barcelona: Barral editores, 1975), p. 14. Quotations in the text come from this edition.

11. Ramón Nieto, *La señorita* (Barcelona: Seix Barral, 1974), p. 9.

12. Janet Díaz, "The Contemporary Novel of Abstract Political Allegory," *American Hispanist* 2, no. 14 (January 1977):4–8.

13. José Ortega, in "Nuevos rumbos en la novelística de posguerra; *Agata, ojo de gato* de Caballero Bonald," *Anales de la novela de posguerra* 2 (1977):19–29.

14. The multiple interpretations, including application to Franco's repressive situation, are suggested in Díaz, *Miguel Delibes,* pp. 150–58.

15. Douglas R. McKay, review of Jesús Torbado, *La construcción del odio, Books Abroad* 43, no. 3 (Summer 1969):385.

16. Gonzalo Torrente Ballester, *La Saga/fuga de J. B.,* 2d ed. (Barcelona: Editorial Destino, 1973), p. 294. Quotations in the text come from this edition.

17. Juan Goytisolo, "Literatura y eutenasia," in *El furgón de cola,* p. 56.

18. Many critics have studied characteristics of language in the new novel in studies of specific authors. For a more general analysis, see Robert Spires, "El nuevo lenguaje de la 'nueva novela,' " *Insula* 396–97 (1979):6–7.

19. The use of the *tú* narrative voice is one of the most characteristic features of the New Novel. An interesting analysis of the effect of its

usage, signaled at a relatively early stage of its usage in Spain, may be seen in Francisco Ynduraín, "La novela desde la segunda persona: análisis estructural," in *Prosa novelesca actual* (Santander: Universidad Internacional Menéndez Pelayo, 1968), pp. 157–82.

20. For example, Alessandro Riccio calls the first two volumes of Luis Goytisolo's *Antagonia,* "no sólo novela, sino ensayo y relato, a la vez," "De las ruinas al taller en la obra de Luis Goytisolo," *Anales de la novela de posguerra* 2 (1977):31.

21. Camilo José Cela, *Oficio de tinieblas 5,* 2d ed. (Barcelona: Editorial Noguer, 1973), p. 7.

22. Manuel Durán addresses the question of musical form in "Vindicación de Juan Goytisolo: *Reivindicación del conde don Julián,*" *Insula* 26 (January 1971):1, 4.

23. Tomás Oguiza, "*Antiliteratura en Oficio de tinieblas, 5* de Camilo José Cela," *Cuadernos hispanoamericanos* 337–38 (July-August 1978):181–87.

24. In a review of Guelbenzu's *Antifaz,* the critic asks, "What is *Antifaz? Antifaz* is a carefree exercise of literary creation. Notice that I am not saying *novel,* because, in the traditional sense of the term, it isn't one." Jorge Rodríguez Padrón, *"Antifaz,* una novela para la polémica," *Cuadernos hispanoamericanos* 85, no. 255 (March 1971):613.

25. Helena Sassone analyzes the "Influencia del barroco en la literatura actual," *Cuadernos hispanoamericanos* 268 (October 1972):147–60.

26. Severo Sarduy, quoted by José Domingo in "Del hermetismo al barroco: Juan Benet y Alfonso Grosso," *Insula* 28 (July-August 1973):20.

27. See, for example, the remarks of José María Castellet in "Panorama literario," in *España perspectiva 1973* (Madrid: Guadiana, 1973), p. 130.

28. Gonzalo Sobejano, "Ante la novela de los años setenta," *Insula* 396–97 (1979):1, 22.

29. For example, Rafael Gómez López Egea, "La novela española en la encrucijada," *Arbor* 90, no. 50 (1975):49–59, laments the lack of communication caused by the literary experiments.

30. Other studies have introduced and analyzed the characteristics of the New Novel and provide a list of names, among them Roberto Saladrigas, "La novela castellana de los años setenta: hacia una ruptura con la guerra civil," *Camp de l'arpa* 48–49 (March 1978):22–25; Janet W. Díaz, "Origins, Aesthetics and the 'Nueva Novela española,' " *Hispania* 59 (March 1979):109–17; Juana Figueras and Argyslas Courage, "La 'nova expressión' narrativa española," *Papeles de Son Armadans* 84 (1977):23–46.

31. Juan Benet, *Volverás a Región* (Barcelona, 1967). Quotations in the text come from this edition.

32. Malcolm Alan Compitello has provided a useful bibliography detailing critical reactions and analyses: "Juan Benet and the Critics," *Anales de la novela de posguerra* 3 (1978):123–41.

33. Pedro Gimferrer, "En torno a *Volverás a Región* de Juan Benet," *Insula* 24 (January 1969):14.

34. Critics have noted Benet's interest in music, particularly in Wagner, whose use of the leitmotif no doubt parallels Benet's literary use of the technique. See Alberto Oliart's review of the novel in *Revista de Occidente* 2ª época, no. 27 (November 1969):224–34. Benet's musical interests are even more apparent in a later work, *Viaje de invierno* (1972), whose title comes from a musical composition by Franz Schubert.

35. David K. Herzberger devotes an excellent section to the portrayal of time in *The Novelistic World of Juan Benet* (Clear Creek, Ind.: The American Hispanist, 1976), pp. 51–56.

36. Luis F. Costa provides some examples of uncertainty and the difficulty of the text in "El lector-viajero en *Volverás a Región*," *Anales de la narrativa española contemporánea* 4 (1979):9–19; David K. Herzberger treats the matter directly in "Enigma as Narrative Determinant in the Novels of Juan Benet."

37. Some excellent examples of readings and misreadings are contained in the Costa article cited in note 36.

38. Interview with Juan Benet, June 1972.

39. Ibid.

40. As acknowledged in his prologue to *La inspiración y el estilo* (Barcelona: Seix Barral, 1973), p. 10. Herzberger mentions many similarities in technique between Proust and Benet in *The Novelistic World of Juan Benet*.

41. For example, see Benet's article "De Canudos a Macondo," *Revista de Occidente* 2ª época, no. 24 (January 1969):49–57.

42. See, for example, Janet Winecoff Díaz, "Spain's Senior 'New Novelist,' Juan Benet," *Studies in Languages and Literature: Proceedings of the 23rd Mountain Interstate Foreign Language Conference* (Richmond: Eastern Kentucky University, 1976), pp. 137–42.

43. The tribute of Ricardo Gullón in "La novela española del siglo XX," *Insula* 34 (November-December 1979):28.

44. Juan Goytisolo, *Reivindicación del conde don Julián,* 2d ed. (Mexico, 1973), p. 52. Quotations in the text come from this edition.

45. Many critics have noted the influence of Martín-Santos on Goytisolo, among them Sobejano, *Novela española de nuestro tiempo,* p. 288, but he acknowledges—as do the others—that Goytisolo goes much further than does Martín-Santos in his experimental techniques.

46. In general, Goytisolo does not take kindly to the Generation of 1898. See, for example, pp. 138–40 in *Reivindicación*.

47. Juan Goytisolo, "Declaración de Juan Goytisolo," *Norte* 13, nos. 4–6 (July-December 1972):91–96.

48. For further comments on the religious element in *Reivindicación,* see the excellent study by Linda G. Levine, "La aniquilación del catolicismo en '*Reivindicación del conde don Julián,*' " *Norte* 13, nos. 4–6 (July-December 1972):133–41.

49. Robert C. Spires provides an excellent analysis of the modern version of the mytheme in his *La novela española de posguerra.*

50. One healthy sign of the recognition of Goytisolo's place in literature can be seen in the growing number of critical works analyzing his work. Some other book-length studies not mentioned above include Linda Gould Levine, *Juan Goytisolo: La destrucción creadora* (Mexico: Editorial Joaquin Mortiz, 1976); Gonzalo Navajas, *La novela de Juan Goytisolo* (Madrid: Sociedad general española de librería, 1979); José Ortega, *Juan Goytisolo (Alienación y agresión en Señas de identidad y Reivindicación del conde don Julián)* (New York: Eliseo Torres & Sons, 1972); Genaro J. Pérez, *Formalist Elements in the Novels of Juan Goytisolo* (Madrid: Ediciones José Porrúa Turranzas, 1979); Hector R. Romero, *La evolución literaria de Juan Goytisolo* (Miami: Ediciones Universal, 1979); and a collection of essays entitled *Juan Goytisolo* (Madrid: Espiral, 1975).

Chapter Ten

1. The return of the exiles and the interest in their place in Hispanic culture have given rise to a series of critical works. The earliest book-length literary study is José R. Marra López, *Narrativa española fuera de España (1939–1961)* (Madrid, 1963); a later series concerning many aspects of the problem is *El exilio español de 1939,* ed. José Luis Abellán, 6 vols. (Madrid: Taurus, 1976–1978). The one most pertinent to this study is vol. 4: *Cultura y literatura,* 1977.

2. In the words of Ignacio Soldevila-Durante, "In our understanding, and surely in that of posterity, the writers and critics who were generational companions of the exiles, who knew of their existence and their publications perfectly well and silenced them for the new generations who looked for an example and guide in them, these people contributed in an unpardonable way to their literary isolation." "La novela española actual," *Revista hispánica moderna* 33 (1967):95.

3. Francisco Ayala, *Los ensayos, teoría y crítica literaria* (Madrid: Aguilar, 1972), pp. 138–64.

4. For example, Sanz Villanueva, "La narrativa del exilio," in *El exilio español de 1939,* 4:114–18.

5. The grouping of Antonio Ferres and José Ortega, *Literatura española del último exilio* (New York: Gordian Press, 1975), p. 8.

6. Paul Ilie, *Literature and Inner Exile: Authoritarian Spain, 1939–1975* (Baltimore and London: The Johns Hopkins University Press, 1980).

Selected Bibliography

PRIMARY SOURCES

Agustí, Ignacio. *Mariona Rebull.* 9th ed. Barcelona: Editorial Destino, 1953.

Benet, Juan. *Volverás a Región.* Barcelona: Editorial Destino, 1967.

Caballero Bonald, J. M. *Dos días de setiembre.* 2d ed. Barcelona: Seix Barral, 1967.

Cela, Camilo José. *La colmena.* 8th ed. Madrid: Noguer, 1967.

―――. *La familia de Pascual Duarte.* Edited by Harold L. Boudreau and John W. Kronik. New York: Appleton-Century-Crofts, 1961.

―――. *Viaje a la Alcarria.* Madrid: Espasa-Calpe, 1961.

Delibes, Miguel. *Cinco horas con Mario.* 4th ed. Barcelona: Editorial Destino, 1969.

Fernández Santos, Jesús. *Los bravos.* Valencia: Editorial Castalia, 1954.

Goytisolo, Juan. *Reivindicación del conde don Julián.* 2d ed. Mexico: Ed. Joaquín Mortiz, S.A., 1973.

Laforet, Carmen. *Nada.* 13th ed. Barcelona: Editorial Destino, 1960.

López Salinas, Armando. *La mina.* Barcelona: Editorial Destino, 1960.

Martín-Santos, Luis. *Tiempo de silencio.* 6th ed. Barcelona: Seix Barral, 1969.

Matute, Ana María. *Primera memoria.* Barcelona: Editorial Destino, 1960.

Sánchez Ferlosio, Rafael. *El Jarama.* 8th ed. Barcelona: Editorial Destino, 1967.

Zunzunegui, Juan A. de. *La vida como es.* Barcelona: Noguer, 1954.

SECONDARY SOURCES

This highly selective list mentions some representative works that present a general view of the contemporary Spanish novel from a developmental or theoretical perspective. Those interested in pursuing the subject in greater depth may consult the annual bibliography of the Publications of the Modern Language Association or the more specialized bibliography in *Anales de la literatura española contemporánea.*

1. Books

Alvarez Palacios, Fernando. *Novela y cultura española de postguerra.* Madrid: Editorial Cuadernos para el diálogo, S.A., 1975. A brief look at various aspects of postwar literature, including exiles and Spanish American influence.

Bosch, Rafael. *La novela española del siglo XX.* New York: Las Americas, 1970. Vol. 2: De la República a la postguerra. Deals primarily with novelistic interpretations of realism, followed by brief analyses of individual works.

Buckley, Ramón. *Problemas formales en la novela española contemporánea.* Barcelona: Ed. Península, 1968. A fine study of selected movements and authorial point of view.

Corrales Egea, José. *La novela española actual.* Madrid: Cuadernos para el diálogo, 1971. Traces the development of the novel through the "contraola" (i.e., the New Novel). Provides a useful comparative chronology of major works from France, Spain, Italy, and Portugal.

Curutchet, Juan Carlos. *Introducción a la novela de postguerra.* Montevideo: Editorial Alfa, 1966. Concentrates on the Mid-Century Generation and its interest in realism and society; chapters devoted to Goytisolo and Fernández-Santos.

Domingo, José. *La novela española del siglo XX.* 2 vols. Barcelona: Ed. Labor, 1973. Useful chronological overview.

Ferreras, Juan Ignacio. *Tendencias de la novela española actual (1931–1969).* Paris: Ed. Hispanoamericanas, 1970. Places particular emphasis on realism. Divided by years: 1940–50, 1950–57, 1957–69.

García-Viñó, Manuel. *Novela española actual.* Madrid: Ed. Guadarrama, 1967. A spokesman for the experimental, intellectual novel, García Viñó offers analyses of works not associated with the social novel.

———. *Novela española de posguerra.* Madrid: Publicaciones españolas, 1971. A chronological treatment, with brief analysis of representative authors.

Gil Casado, Pablo. *La novela social española.* 2d ed. Barcelona: Editorial Seix Barral, 1973. A useful study, with theoretical introduction and thematic presentation.

Guillermo, Edenia, and **Hernández, Juana Amelia.** *La novelística española de los sesenta.* New York: Eliseo Torres and Sons, 1971. A concise useful introduction to the postwar novel, with analyses of novels representing postneorealism.

Hickey, Leo. *Realidad y experiencia de la novela.* Madrid: CUPSA Editorial, 1978. Moves from general theoretical premises (the novel and empirical reality, novel in a social context, etc.) to the novel and Spanish culture, ending with a section on five contemporary Spanish novelists.

Iglesias Laguna, Antonio. *Treinta años de novela española (1938–1968)*. Madrid: Ed. Prensa Española, 1970. Particular emphasis on various categories of realism during this period. Treats a large number of novelists.

Marra-López, José R. *Narrativa española fuera de España (1939–1961)*. Madrid: Ed. Guadarrama, 1963. A first section deals with literature between 1920 and 1936, followed by characteristics of the exiled writer and analyses of the works of the more prominent exiled prose writers.

Martínez-Cachero, J. M. *Historia de la novela española entre 1939 y 1969*. Madrid: Ed. Castalia, 1973. Interesting for the material describing postwar cultural factors as they affect the literature of the period. Excellent critical bibliography.

Morán, Fernando. *Explicación de una limitación: la novela realista de los años cincuenta en España*. Madrid: Taurus, 1971. Explains neorealism in terms of its historical environment.

———. *Novela y semidesarrollo*. Madrid: Ed. Taurus, 1971. A penetrating study tying literary development to changing socioeconomic conditions.

Nora, Eugenio G. de. *La novela española contemporánea (1939–1967)*. 2d ed. Madrid: Ed. Gredos, 1971. One of the basic works on this period; offers analyses of major novels, often brief remarks on minor novels.

Roberts, Gemma. *Temas existenciales en la novela de postguerra*. Madrid: Ed. Gredos, 1973. A brief introduction concerning existentialism and contemporary Spanish literature; analysis of four major themes applied to four novels.

Sanz Villanueva, Santos. *Historia de la novela social española (1942–1975)*. 2 vols. Madrid: Editorial Alhambra, 1980. A thorough study of background and development followed by analyses of authors grouped by stylistic or critical affinities.

———. *Tendencies de la novela española actual (1950–1970)*. Madrid: Cuadernos para el diálogo, 1972. Develops the content-form relationship with particular emphasis on experimentation and change.

Sobejano, Gonzalo. *Novela española de nuestro tiempo (en busca del pueblo perdido)*. 2d ed. Madrid: Ed. Prensa española, 1975. Excellent study dividing the novel into three rough groupings: existential, social, and structural.

Soldevila-Durante, Ignacio. *La novela desde 1936*. Madrid: Editorial Alhambra, 1980. An extremely detailed and helpful study that briefly outlines the work of many major and minor novelists.

Spires, Robert C. *La novela española de posguerra: creación artística y experiencia personal*. Madrid: CUPSA, 1978. A fine study connecting the postwar novel with the spirit of the times. Analyses from the point of view of the implicit reader's relationship with the text.

Villanueva, Darío. *Estructura y tiempo reducido en la novela.* Valencia: Editorial Bello, 1977. An excellent, well-documented study with numerous examples from the Spanish novel.

————. *El Jarama de Sánchez Ferlosio: su estructura y significado.* Santiago: Universidad de Santiago de Compostela, 1973. The first half is a thorough study of the characteristics and development of the Mid-Century Generation.

Yerro Villanueva, Tomás. *Aspectos técnicos y estructurales de la novela española actual.* Pamplona: Eunsa, 1977. An introduction outlining the postwar evolution followed by analyses of four characteristic techniques of the New Novel applied to four works.

2. Articles

Buckley, Ramón. "Del realismo social al realismo dialéctico." *Insula,* no. 326 (1974):1, 4. Divides the postwar novel into three stages (existential-tremendista; neorealism; dialectical realism).

Castellet, José María. "Veinte años de novela española (1942–1962)." *Cuadernos Americanos* 126 (February 1963):290–95. Divides novelists into two "generations" (critical realism and historical realism).

Díaz, Janet W. "Origins, Aesthetics and the *Nueva novela española."* *Hispania* 59 (1976):109–17. An informative introduction to the New Novel; includes characteristics, names, and works.

Domingo, José. " 'Novisimos,' 'Nuevos' y 'renovados.' " *Insula,* no. 316 (March 1973):6. Attempts to classify the authors writing "New Novels."

Figueras, Juana y Argyslas Courage. "La 'nova expressión' narrativa española." *Papeles de Son Armandans* 250 (January 1977):23–46. Points out the characteristics of and influences on the most experimental novelists.

Ortega, José. "Nuevas direcciones en los novelistas españoles de la 'Generación de medio siglo.' " *Norte* 13, nos. 4–6 (1972):87–90. Traces the changes from neorealism to psychological or linguistic interests in these novelists.

Winecoff, Janet. "The Spanish Novel from Ortega to Castellet: Dehumanization of the Artist." *Hispania* 50 (March 1967):35–43. A fine article discussing the theories behind neorealism, particularly objectivism.

Index